When Everyone Else Zigs...

ZAG

THE POWER OF THINKING DIFFERENTLY

MICHAEL CLAWSON

I0394768

Copyright © 2017 by Michael Clawson

All rights reserved.
No part of this book may be used or reproduced in any manner whatsoever except for brief quotations in critical reviews without express written consent of the author.

ISBN-13: 978-1543001792

ISBN-10: 1543001793

For Meghan, Anna, Ben, and Brandon

Contents

Part One: Zag?
1. Life in the Shoal 11
2. Zig-Zag 16

Part Two: Inertia
3. Objects at Rest 23
4. Hardwired 31
5. The Hot Hand 38
6. Hobgoblins 44
7. Maginot 52
8. Past Performance 60
9. Shift 67
10. A New Model(s) 73
11. Finding Longitude 78

Part Three: Risk
12. Protect and Thrive 89
13. Decisions, Decisions 93
14. Insurance? 98
15. The Paradox of Inaction 105
16. Green Revolution 110
17. Ambush 116
18. Go for it! 123
19. Burn the Boats 130
20. We Choose the Moon 135

Part Four: Culture
21. Second Nature 143
22. Superior Orders 148

23. Manmade Disasters 158
24. Cultural Advantage 166
25. Cultural Advantage v2.0 170
26. Spirit of Competition 175
27. Rosa and the Rest of the Story 183

Part Five: Information
28. Murky Water 194
29. Thin Slice 198
30. Drowning in Data 213
31. Operation Bodyguard 220
32. The Boy Who Lived 226
33. Page Rank 231
34. Reversing the Curse 237
35. A Cautionary Tale 251

Part Six: Conformity
36. No Soap Radio! 261
37. Madness & Hysteria 266
38. The Selfish Herd 275
39. Three Men Make a Tiger 283
40. Consensus at Any Cost 289
41. The Devil's Advocate 294
42. How Vasili Arkhipov Saved the World 299

Part Seven: Parting Shots
43. Good Isn't Bad 313
44. The Path to Greatness 318

Acknowledgements

ZAG

THE POWER OF THINKING DIFFERENTLY

Part One

Zag?

CHAPTER 1

LIFE IN THE SHOAL

*"Two roads diverged in a wood, and I –
I took the one less traveled by,
And that has made all the difference."*

– *The Road Not Taken* by Robert Frost

One of the world's most spectacular natural phenomena commences in the treacherous waters off the southern tip of South Africa. It begins in the Agulhas Bank, an ocean region where the cold waters of the Atlantic Ocean converge with the warm waters of the Indian Ocean creating turbulent water that churns up nutrients from the ocean depths. The abundance of nutrients combined with cool water creates ideal conditions for tiny aquatic plants called phytoplankton to bloom and flourish. Phytoplankton serves a critical role in numerous marine food chains, including supplying the primary source of food for *Sardinops sagax*, the South American pilchard, a fish more commonly known as a sardine. In these tumultuous waters teeming with life, the sardines begin their fateful journey.

The sardine's 2-3 year life span begins in the Agulhas Bank when adult sardines spawn in the spring and summer months. After spawning, fertilized eggs drift north along the West coast of Africa where they hatch and begin to mature. Once the young sardines gain enough strength, they aggregate into massive groups called shoals and head southward returning to the Agulhas Bank. The sardines instinctively form and then spend most of their lives in giant shoals. For nearly its entire life, a single sardine reaps great benefit from membership in the collective.

Scientists believe that shoals provide foraging advantages, grant increased access to potential mates, improve swimming efficiency, and frequently confer protection from predators. By living together in shoals and by doing everything the same as every other member of the group, a single sardine can greatly improve its life. However, for many of these sardines, a fateful day approaches when their instinct to stay close to one another will ultimately result in their demise.

Between May and July, when the water temperature drops to the right level, the great sardine shoals begin their epic run. For reasons not completely understood by modern science, the sardines commence a migration northward along the Eastern coast of Africa. The largest shoals can measure four miles long, one mile wide, and 100 feet deep. Countless shoals stretch along the African coastline each bursting with life.

Each shoal contains millions of sardines that together look like colossal silvery shimmering clouds. Strung together, the individual shoals comprise "the great sardine run." Scientists estimate the migration contains biomass on par with East Africa's great wildebeest migration.* The sheer numbers of the glistening shoals attract a remarkable variety of predators which assemble en-masse off the coastline in advance of the great sardine run. This congregation sets the stage for one of the most dramatic events in the natural world.

As the massive shoals of sardines migrate northward, many species of predators gather in anticipation of the feeding frenzy about to ensue. Pods of common and bottlenose dolphins typically consisting of 10-50 members aggregate into super-pods several thousand strong. Scores of sharks including great whites, hammerheads, bronze whalers, and blacktips assemble and await the arrival of the great shoals of baitfish. Large predatory fish such as king mackerel and blue tuna along with throngs of sea birds including dive-bombing cape gannets rush to partake in the feast. Massive brown fur seals waddle off their sandy seaside perches on the West coast of Africa to pursue the shoals northward and join in the fray. The imminent confluence of the great sardine shoals and the eclectic mix of marine predators results in one of the most marvelous and electrifying events in nature.

---

*Biomass refers to the total mass of living matter within a given area. Accordingly, the weight of all the sardines in the great sardine run roughly equals the weight of all the wildebeests in the great wildebeest migration. If one considers that wildebeests weigh between 265-600lbs each and an estimated 1.5 million participate in the migration, one can better appreciate the incredible number of sardines that comprise the great sardine run.

The thrilling attack features an astonishing display of cooperation among predators. The dolphins lead the assault, cutting violently though the swarming shoal and slicing it into smaller sections. Once threatened by the dolphins, the instincts that bound individual sardines to the shoal intensify driving the sardines even more tightly together.

The crafty and cooperative dolphins use this instinct against the unwitting sardines. They continue to slice the shoal into massive bait balls that can reach up to 70 feet in diameter. Each bait ball swarms with densely packed and frenzied sardines all swimming progressively tighter together attempting to escape the attack from the circling dolphins. Acting like sheep dogs, the dolphins team to coral the bait ball, keeping it intact as the other predators prepare to launch their own attack.

The bait ball will last less than 20 frenetic minutes with relatively few sardines surviving the flurry of attacks. Sharks fire into the bait ball, mouths gaping wide, gorging themselves. Simultaneously, several species of predatory fishes shoot through the bait ball from multiple directions devouring fish with every pass. Seals join in the tumult and dart in and out snaring sardines. Then, from above, the cape gannets plunge from the sky striking the water at speeds exceeding 60 miles per hour propelling themselves deep into the swarm. The predators' furious assault will not relent until they consume the entire bait ball.

For an individual sardine, the instinct to join the shoal and follow every other sardine served it well for most of its life. The shoal brought it food and safety. The shoal provided it with access to mates and made swimming easier. However, on this fateful day, following the shoal led the sardine directly into a death trap.

For its entire life, the individual sardine followed the shoal. When the shoal moved left, the sardine moved left. When the shoal moved right, the sardine moved right. When the shoal zigged, the sardine zigged. However, on this final day, at this critical juncture, the individual sardine would have survived if it broke from the shoal. When the shoal zigged, the sardine should have zagged.

CHAPTER 2

ZIG-ZAG

"He who joyfully marches to music in rank and file has already earned my contempt. He has been given a large brain by mistake, since for him the spinal cord would fully suffice."

— Albert Einstein

A single sardine doesn't have the ability to zag when the shoal zigs. Bound by its nature, a sardine must spend its entire life in the shoal. Innate and unlearned fixed action patterns called instincts govern animal behavior. Instinct causes the sardines to shoal, drives wildebeests to migrate, and compels sea turtles to move towards the ocean once hatched.

In many ways, humans aren't a whole lot different than sardines. Similar to other animals, innate and unlearned drives influence human behavior. But people have an ability that sardines do not possess – the power of choice. Because individuals can override their instincts and choose to act in opposition to their innate drives, people can accomplish something that the sardines and other animals can never achieve. While sardines must spend their entire life as a captive in the shoal, people possess freedom. Sardines must always follow their instincts and zig, but people have the ability to break free and zag.

To Zig

In the sardine shoal metaphor, "zigging" means mindlessly following the shoal and behaving the same way as every member of the group. For sardines, zigging leads to many benefits, but it also has its limitations. While all shoal members benefit, no shoal member ever ascends to greatness and most perish on the great run.

Translating to human behavior, the concept of zigging applies more broadly and with more complexity, but the core idea remains the same. Zigging can often result in benefit, but it never leads to greatness or progress.

Zigging means doing things the "normal way," the way everyone else does, in a manner that most wouldn't think to question. It means accepting and following the conventional wisdom.

Conventional wisdom accumulates slowly over time, deeply ingraining it into the fabric of societies. As a result, most people tend to follow typical thought patterns without question. They willingly accept the prevailing thinking as truth, and they act in eager accordance with widespread beliefs assumed as fact.

But zigging is not all bad. Zigging is necessary and beneficial. For a society to function properly and its members to thrive, individuals must zig and conform consistently along many dimensions.

Everyone stands a better chance of surviving if everyone agrees to drive on the same side of the road, stop at stop signs, and obey other common driving regulations. Without people consistently following the rule of law and resisting barbarous impulses, societies would devolve into anarchy.

Individuals can reap many benefits from zigging. People gain from the efficiency of taking conventional approaches to solving problems and accomplishing tasks. Conventional approaches capitalize on the cumulative knowledge of society, and more often than not, generate correct decisions and acceptable results. People don't need to reinvent the wheel when the wheel they have works just fine.

But, if one only thinks conventionally and always follows the shoal, he or she will never stand out and achieve individual success. To attain greatness and realize progress, one must occasionally zag.

To Zag

If zigging involves thinking and behaving conventionally, "zagging" means breaking free from convention and choosing to think and act differently. Unlike the sardines that must blindly follow their instincts to shoal, people can choose their own path.

But zagging is hard. To escape the trappings of the conventional, one must overcome the factors that conspire to restrain thinking and impede action. These insidious influences make it incredibly difficult to veer from the conventional path. The efficiency and frequent accuracy of the conventional approach compounds the predicament, making it even more challenging to choose to zag. Why zag, when zigging works most of the time? Why zag, when zigging creates good results?

One zags to achieve greatness, to realize progress, and to win. While zigging generates average outcomes, zagging breeds excellence. Zagging will often fail, but one must zag if he or she ever aspires to ascend above the crowd.

At first blush, zagging might appear similar to simply being a contrarian – when the crowd goes left, simply go right in order to zag. But this misses an essential element of successful zagging. It's what separates true zagging from merely being contrarian. The contrarian's end objective is "to be different," and their strategy is to simply take positions and actions that are in opposition to popular ones. Sometimes they will be proven correct, but it will only be by accident. In contrast to the mere contrarian, the zagger's end objective is "to succeed."

The zagger doesn't mindlessly take the less worn path. Zagging is not haphazard or accidental. The zagger doesn't employ a basic strategy of simply going in the opposite direction. The zagger makes a well-reasoned and informed choice to take the less worn path because they believe it will lead to a desired outcome. Where the contrarian might assume unnecessary risks, the zagger will take calculated risks. More importantly, the zagger won't "zag" all the time. The zagger doesn't always take positions and act differently from the group. They selectively choose to act differently precisely when they believe that acting differently will lead to success.

To zag, one must make a mindful decision to think or act differently with the realistic expectation of superior results. In the sardine metaphor, the contrarian sardine never joins the shoal. On the other hand, the sardine that zags joins the shoal reaping all the benefits of shoal membership. Then, just prior to embarking on the great run, correctly anticipating the death trap ahead, it makes the choice to break from the shoal and survive.

Zig-Zag

Numerous forces conspire to prevent people from zagging, relegating most to an average life in the shoal. This book is organized around 5 of the most powerful forces that compel people to the conventional. It examines how each force drives people to think and act conventionally and tells the stories of both ill-fated zigs and great zags.

Behind every zig, there is a story of someone unable to overcome the powerful drive that bound them to the shoal. Conversely, behind every zag, there is an inspiring tale of someone who overcame those powerful forces, made the choice to think differently, and succeeded. We can learn from both those who failed by zigging and those who succeeded by zagging.

The following is an exploration of those forces that compel humanity to the conventional and the stories behind those ill-fated zigs and great zags…

Part Two

Inertia

CHAPTER 3

OBJECTS AT REST

in·er·tia *i-ˈnər-shə, -shē-ə*\   *A property of matter by which it remains at rest or in uniform motion in the same straight line unless acted upon by some external force*

Born prematurely on Christmas 1642 on a sheep farm in Lincolnshire, England. Isaac Newton would eventually have profound influence every branch of modern science.* Newton's life began rather humbly and inauspiciously as the posthumous son of a yeoman farmer and an absentee mother. An unusually small child, whose mother joked could fit easily inside of a "quart-mug," Newton would eventually stand unparalleled as a scientific giant.

Newton accomplished so much during his career that his work inspired English poet Alexander Pope to pen this now famous epitaph:

Nature and nature's laws lay hid in night;
God said "Let Newton be" and all was light.

---

* Newton was born on December 25, 1642. When England later transitioned from the Julian to the Gregorian calendar, the exact date of his birth adjusted to January 4, 1643.

Before Newton inspired god-like veneration from his contemporaries, he had to change the way people thought about the natural world. Before Newton, the prevailing thinking included theories that people today would consider laughable. And yet, while seemingly silly with the benefit of modern knowledge, leading scientists, universities, and even churches fully espoused these beliefs, deeply ingraining them into the fabric of science and society.

Most associate Newton with his monumental breakthroughs in the areas of gravity and motion. People remember the story of the falling apple and the famous Law of Inertia. In these two areas, contemporary thinking preceding Newton hinged on hypothesizes formulated by Aristotle around 350 BC.

Aristotelian physics postulated that objects move toward different parts of the universe based on their composition of the four primary elements known as Air, Fire, Earth and Water. According to the theory, an object such as an apple consists primarily of the element "Earth" so when it detaches from a tree it moves toward the location in the universe containing the most "Earth."

According to Aristotelian physics, objects would only move away from their natural place when compelled to do so. For example, if a person threw an apple, it would move away from its natural place since the force of the throw compelled it. Aristotelian physics also asserted that motion stops as soon as the compelling force ceases to act. Unless something applies continuous force to the apple, it would fall toward the center of the Earth.

This theory proved problematic for its proponents. For once the apple leaves one's hand, no obvious force continues to push it forward. Physicists hypothesized that movement of the apple thinned the air behind it, creating a temporary vacuum that compelled the apple forward until it eventually fell toward its "natural place."

Newton challenged widely held views that persisted for two millennia, and forever changed the way people thought about the world. No longer do apples fall to Earth because of a tendency toward a "natural place." No longer does the apple continue to move through the air because of a vacuum that continues to exert a compelling force. Because of Newton, the world knows that the apple falls because of Gravity, and that the apple continues to move once thrown because of Inertia.

Newton codified these theories in his epic monograph *Principles*.* In this masterwork, Newton completely rewrote humankind's understanding of the natural world. Perhaps most impressively, in postulating and developing his theories for *Principles*, Newton, limited by the mathematical theories of the day, conceived a new form of mathematics later known as Calculus to help him complete his work. Taken together, these monumental scientific advances laid

---

* The full title, in Latin, *Philosophiæ Naturalis Principia Mathematica* translates to "Mathematical Principles of Natural Philosophy" and was originally published on July 5, 1687.

the foundation for Classical Mechanics which would dominate scientific thinking in the field of Physics for nearly three centuries.*

In developing and writing *Principles,* Newton eschewed conventional thinking, forever changed the way people thought about the world, and achieved fantastic success. Despite his accomplishments, Newton remained humble asserting, "If I have seen further it is by standing on the shoulders of giants."

However, even Newton, in all his genius, might not have anticipated that his groundbreaking work in Physics would offer such a compelling paradigm in the cognitive sciences. While Sir Isaac Newton's Laws of Motion accurately describe how physical objects behave in the natural world, when applied to the concept of human thought and behavior, they provide a compelling explanation for why people tend to think conventionally.

To illustrate, let's try a little experiment. Take a look at the following set of arrows and judge for yourself which line is longer:

---

* Classical Mechanics including Gravity and the Laws of Motion endure to this day; however, there are limitations in Newton's thinking with objects that are extremely small or move extremely fast. These special cases require Quantum and Relativistic mechanics to resolve. Newton's law accurately describes motion within "Newtonian" or "Inertial" reference frames, but as objects approach the speed of light, Einstein's concepts of relativity are required to accurately explain the natural world.

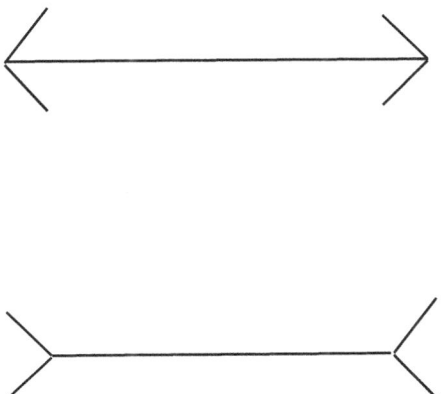

In all likelihood, you already know the answer. During your life, you have probably encountered this or similar perspective-based illusions numerous times.* You learned that our visual system perceives and analyzes depth and distance in a way that seamlessly adjusts for angles and perspective allowing us to efficiently interpret and maneuver effectively in a three-dimensional world. You know how this illusion exploits that great human capability. You know this trick. You have seen it before – many times. Or have you?

The illustration on the following page reveals the truth.

---

* This is known as the Müller-Lyer illusion.

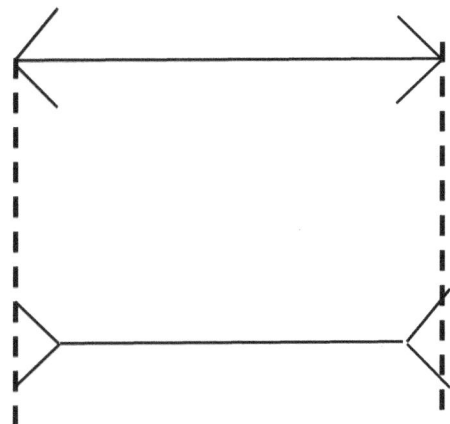

This time the lines are not the same length. In fact, the top line is 25% longer than the bottom line.

This is a different trick and it exploits another great human capability. Humans learn quickly and retain knowledge exceptionally well. Sometime in grammar school, a teacher probably exposed you to the Müller-Lyer illusion. The illusion fooled you the first time – but you learned. Later in life, you probably came across the same illusion a few more times, but each time you knew the trick. You applied that same knowledge, again and again. And you were proven correct every time. This time you applied the same answer, but the question changed in a subtle, but important, way.

Now, let's try another one. This time instead of a visual system test, let's examine your auditory system with a simple spelling test. The following contains a series of spelling questions. Please answer them <u>out loud</u>.

Question 1: Spell "Hop"
> *Please answer out loud:*   H-O-P

Question 2: Spell "Mop"
> *Please answer out loud:*   M-O-P

Question 3: Spell "Top"
> *Please answer out loud:*   T-O-P

Question 4: What do you do at a green light?
> *Please answer out loud....*

Did you answer "Stop"? The answer is not "Stop." You "Go" at a green light. Accustomed to hearing and processing the "op" sound, many continue the pattern and answer the easy question incorrectly.*

Some will get this simple question correct. After the visual trick with the lines, these people will approach the spelling test with caution. Even with vigilance, they probably will have to resist the urge to answer "Stop." Faced with a question that in isolation a young child would easily answer correctly, highly intelligent and highly vigilant people often struggle.

But the question is not asked in isolation. It is asked in a context that creates momentum, and momentum is difficult to overcome. Whether it's visual, like the lines, or

---

* You may remember similar riddles from your days on the playground. If you are interested, these are my other favorites: #1: Questions - Spell "Roast"; Spell "Toast"; Spell "Most". What do you put in a toaster? Answer: Bread, of course. #2 Questions – Spell "Folk"; Spell "Joke"; Spell "Poke". What's the white of an egg called? Answer: Albumen, not Yolk.

auditory, like the spelling test, Newton's Law of Inertia applies.

Why?

Because thoughts and actions are just like objects. When they get put into motion, they tend to stay in motion. Inertia exerts its powerful influence without prejudice in both the mental and physical worlds.

Newton's Law of Inertia governs all – thoughts, objects, actions – nothing is immune. For, in addition to serving as the First Law of Motion, Inertia also serves as the First Driver of Zigging.

CHAPTER 4

HARDWIRED

"He who is fixed to a star does not change his mind."

– Leonardo da Vinci

Mental Inertia exerts a powerful and pervasive force on people's thoughts and actions. Its ubiquitous influence stems from a powerful predilection hardwired directly into every human brain.

To demonstrate, examine the checkerboard developed by Edward H. Adelson, Professor of Vision Science at MIT:

Edward H. Adelson

Now ask yourself, which square is darker – the one labeled "A" or "B"? Clearly, the square labeled A appears darker, but in reality, the squares are exactly the same color. A slight modification provides some clarity.

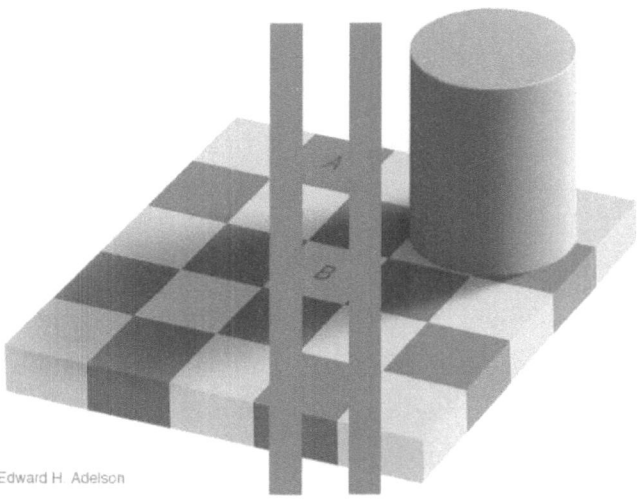

Edward H. Adelson

In this image, with the assistance of the connecting lines, one can see that the two blocks are the same color.

Adelson's checkerboard belongs to a class of illusions known as color consistency illusions. In these types of illusions, the brain changes the color it perceives based on assumptions about the surroundings. In this case, the brain expects the color pattern of a checkerboard with alternating light and dark squares and the darkening effect of a shadow.

As a result, the brain changes how it interprets the stimuli received from the optic nerve causing one to see a color difference that doesn't exist. The brain expects a checkerboard pattern, so the brain perceives a checkerboard pattern, even when it isn't there.

Optical illusions provide informative glimpses into the inner workings of the human mind. Illusions like this one occur because of people's unconscious inferences about the world. These mental shorthands make perceiving and understanding a complicated world a lot more efficient.

Color consistency allows humans to quickly recognize objects regardless of lighting, an incredibly valuable skill. In this example, the brain makes an unconscious inference, a simplifying assumption about the world, that the checkerboard will have alternating light and dark squares. Most of the time, the brain's simplifying assumptions will be correct, just not this time.

Now, flip back a few pages for a moment and look at the first image again. Can you see that the squares are the same color?

You still can't see it? Square B still appears lighter, right? Don't be too hard on yourself. If you want to blame anything, blame your genetics that have hardwired inertia directly into your brain.

Some scuba divers experience an interesting and related phenomenon. As they progress deeper underwater, divers should lose the ability to see color. Water absorbs the longest wavelength, lowest frequency colors first. Reds and oranges disappear completely between 15-25 feet of water followed by yellow, green, blue, and violet. Depending on water clarity, all color disappears at depths of 200-300 feet. Despite the fact that no human can physically observe color at certain depths, many divers report spotting brilliantly colored fish at levels far below where they should be able to see color.

Seeing the impossible flummoxes veteran divers who understand they have observed something that defies the laws of physics. In reality, no law of physics has been broken. The diver, who knows exactly what the fish should look like, perceives the fish consistently with his or her preexisting expectations. Just like the checkerboard example, the diver expects to see a colorful fish, and perceives one, despite the physical inability to observe color.

Once the brain has an expectation, despite stimuli, and even proof to the contrary, the brain maintains that expectation. That expectation will shape perception. It won't change easily. An object in motion will continue in motion. An object at rest will stay at rest.

Color consistency illusions demonstrate the innate process by which mental inertia affects how people perceive their environment. This form of mental inertia helps the brain simplify a complicated world, but as the Adelson illusion demonstrates, it doesn't always work perfectly.

Anchoring

Mental inertia not only effects visual perception, it also has a pervasive influence on judgment. A cognitive bias known as anchoring exerts constant, but undetected, pressure on decision making. With anchoring, a single piece of previously acquired information or experience known as the "anchor" shapes the way humans make decisions. Like color consistency, anchoring often results in efficient decision making, but it can lead to incorrect decisions biased by completely irrelevant information.

Play along with this classic anchoring example by answering the following questions:

1. Do you think the Mississippi River is shorter or longer than 500 miles?
2. How many miles long is the Mississippi River?

Most people answer "longer" to the first question, and the average response to the second question is typically around 1,000 miles.

Now, try again, this time with just one small change made to the questions:

1. Do you think the Mississippi River is shorter or longer than 5,000 miles?
2. How many miles long is the Mississippi River?

Respondents given the second set of questions typically answer "shorter" to the first question, but their average response to the second question increases to about 2,000 miles.*

---

* The Mississippi river is 2,320 miles long making it the 4th largest in the world behind the Nile, Amazon, and Yangtze.

The 500 and 5,000 function as anchors drawing the average response toward them. A seemingly innocuous initial question plants an anchor in the respondent's mind creating an inertial force that influences the answer to the second question.

In this example, the anchors directly relate to the second question, and the choice of 500 and 5,000 appear perfectly reasonable in context. However, the anchoring bias occurs even with completely arbitrary anchors.

In their seminal work on anchoring, Amos Tversky and Daniel Kahneman created an anchor by spinning a "wheel of fortune" in a test subject's presence. The wheel generated completely random numbers between zero and 100. After the number was generated, researchers asked test subjects if the percentage of African countries in the United Nations was higher or lower than that random number. Then they asked their subjects to guess the actual percentage of African countries in the United Nations.

Like in the Mississippi River example, the anchor biased the subject's response in the direction of the anchor. Those who got a 10 on the wheel of fortune offered median estimates of 25% and those who had a 65 on the wheel had a median estimate of 45%. In this case, the anchor, albeit transparently random to the test subject, still exerted a powerful inertial force on their decision making.*

---

* At time of this printing, African countries comprised 28% of the UN member states (54 out of 193) making the African group the largest contingent of the 5 major groups just ahead of the Asia-Pacific group (53).

A recent study with Stanford undergraduates shows that the anchoring bias impacts decision making with a cross-modal anchor. In the previous two examples, a numerical anchor biased a numerical estimate. In the Stanford study, researchers added a unique twist to the classic Mississippi River experiment.

In the experiment, researchers asked students to replicate three lines without the use of a ruler. Some students received lines that measured 1 inch and others got ones that measured 3.5 inches. After drawing the lines, the students were asked to estimate the length of the Mississippi River. Researchers found that students who drew long lines estimated the river to measure much longer than those who drew short lines. The researchers conducted additional experiments all leading to the same conclusion: physical anchors can bias a numerical estimate. Anchoring's powerful influence extends across modalities.

Most people think and act completely oblivious to the strong inertial forces that innate biases like anchoring exert on their decision-making. Anchoring tethers and limits judgment preventing the mind from acting nimbly and freely to make unbiased decisions. Because of this instinctive bias, existing information and paradigms exert undue influence on future thinking. Like objects at rest tend to stay at rest, minds with anchors tend to be biased toward the anchor. Mental inertia is hardwired.

CHAPTER 5

THE HOT HAND

"Prediction is very difficult, especially if it's about the future."

– Niels Bohr

Most think of inertia as a static force that tethers people's thoughts to a fixed position. But Newton's law applies more broadly. Not only do objects at rest tend to stay at rest, objects in motion tend to stay in motion. The second half of the law applies equal force. It often exerts its invisible but powerful influence when people encounter streaks or trends. Like an inertial anchor biases thinking toward the anchor, inertia sustains momentum encouraging thinking to continue in the direction of the trend.

Imagine this scenario. In the decisive Game 7 of the NBA finals, your favorite team has trailed by 10 or more points for most of the night.* Then, late in the game,

---

* For those who aren't basketball fans, the NBA is the National Basketball Association, the most popular professional basketball league on the planet. The NBA finals pits the two conference champions against each other in a best of 7 game series to decide the NBA champion. The winner of game 7 would be crowned the NBA champion.

sparked by some very hot shooting by one of your guards, your team mounts a tremendous comeback. Your guard, usually just an average shooter is "on fire." He just made his 8th consecutive shot pulling your team within one point of the lead. After getting a stop on defense, your team gets possession of the ball back with time for one final shot. Your coach calls a time out to set up a final play. This final shot will determine the NBA champion.

Should the coach design a play to get an open shot for the guard on an incredible hot streak? Of course, he should, right? This guy can't miss. He is on fire. He has the hot hand!

Guess again. The hot hand is just a myth.

In 1985, three well-respected researchers published a paper that offered a surprising conclusion.[*] They conducted a detailed analysis using shots taken during live action in NBA games (Philadelphia 76ers), free throws attempted during NBA contests (Boston Celtics), and controlled shooting experiments with both male and female college basketball players (Cornell University). The researchers meticulously combed through the data. They ran correlation after correlation. As hard as they tried, they couldn't find evidence of the "hot hand" or "streak shooting."

The metaphor of coin flipping illustrates their point. After enough flips of a coin, there will be sequences when

---

[*] Thomas Gilovich (Cornell University), Robert Vallone (Stanford University), and Amos Tversky (Stanford University). The paper was titled "The Hot Hand in Basketball: On the Misperception of Random Sequences."

heads comes up 5 times in a row. Similarly, if a player makes 50% of his shots, sometimes he will make 5 shots in a row. But that doesn't mean he is on a hot shooting streak any more than the person who flips 5 consecutive heads is on a hot coin-flipping streak. Despite the fact that making a basketball shot requires significant skill, the chance of making a given shot is independent of making or missing the previous shot.

Even though the data suggests otherwise, the authors found that fans almost universally believe in streak shooting. They found that a staggering 91% of fans think a player has a better chance of making his next shot after making two or three in a row versus missing two or three in a row. And 84% of fans said that teammates should pass the ball to the player who has made consecutive shots. If confronted with the hypothetical situation at the beginning of this chapter, the average fan would almost certainly design the play for the guard on the hot streak.

Since the authors published their pioneering research, many have debated the study's conclusions. Some critiqued the sample size and others questioned the methodology. Many developed alternative studies and leveraged different data sets in a quest to find evidence of the hot hand. Despite great effort, researchers have consistently failed to prove the hot hand's existence. If there is such a thing as a hot hand in sports, it is fleeting at best and incredibly elusive to isolate in the data with any level of certainty.

However, for understanding the inescapable influence of mental inertia, the most interesting question is not whether a basketball player occasionally gets the "hot hand" or goes on a shooting "streak." And it doesn't really matter what fans believe. It matters what players believe and what actions they take as a result.

Do players believe in the hot hand? Do they believe that a made shot means they are more likely to make the next one? Do the results of the past predict the future? And, what do players do about it?

Two researchers, John Huizinga and Sandy Weil, set out to answer some of these questions. They utilized an extensive data set using four complete seasons of NBA games – over 200 times the data used in the original study. They made adjustments to their methodology to account for the critiques of the original work. With more and better data and a more sophisticated methodology, Huizinga and Weil reached a similar, but slightly different conclusion.

While players, coaches, and fans almost universally believe in streak shooting, they found if a player made a shot, their field goal percentage on the next shot actually went down. Not only did they find no evidence that the hot hand exists, they found that the opposite is true.

They found that after a made shot, the player is more likely to miss the next shot. According to the data, the average player makes 46.7% of their field goal attempts after a missed shot. But, following a made shot, the percentage drops to just 43.2%. The surprising results directly contradict the conventional wisdom.

But how can this be? As it turns out, NBA players, biased by mental inertia, believe in the hot hand, and they act accordingly. Following a made shot, NBA players shoot more quickly, more frequently, and they attempt increasingly difficult shots.

The researchers found that following a made jump shot, NBA players attempted their next shot 47.3 seconds of game time later. If the player missed a jump shot, they waited 56.5 seconds to attempt their next one. Following a made shot, NBA players shoot 9.2 seconds or 16% faster. Over the course of a 48-minute NBA game, that can translate to lot of extra shots.

And those extra shots tend to come at the expense of shots from other players on the team. Following a made shot, a player attempts the team's next shot 34% of the time. Following a missed shot, they only attempt the team's next shot 26% of the time.

Players also tend to attempt more difficult shots following a made attempt. The data showed that after a player makes a long shot (i.e., jump shot), that player will shoot another jump shot about 85% of the time on their next attempt. If the player misses a jump shot, they only attempt another jump shot 77% of the time with their subsequent shot. Confidence from the made shot, leads to more long shots. Following a miss, the player's confidence dips, and they tend to attempt easier shots like layups and dunks.

Buoyed by their belief in the hot hand, NBA players display significant overconfidence following a made shot. They shoot much faster, more frequently, and they attempt more difficult shots. And this overconfidence negatively impacts the team. The researchers calculated these poor decisions cost the team an average of 1.8 points per game.

Extrapolating over an entire season, these poor decisions, based on the assumption of a hot hand, would cost the team between 4-5 victories per year.

The basketball players making poor shot decisions have succumbed to the forces of mental inertia. Propelled by the momentum in the direction of the trend, players grow overconfident, and their poor decisions cost their team points and games.

What if one team eschewed the conventional thinking and didn't fall victim to the hot hand myth? What if while everyone else zigged, one team zagged? That team would probably win a few extra games every year, perhaps enough to help them make the playoffs, perhaps enough to propel them to a championship.

CHAPTER 6

HOBGOBLINS

"A foolish consistency is the hobgoblin of little minds, adored by little statesmen and philosophers and divines."

— Ralph Waldo Emerson

Basketball players get caught up in the momentum and inertia propels them in the direction of the trend. The NBA player makes many decisions in a short time. The impact of their decisions translates to results quickly as well. Shots are made or missed. Games are won or lost.

But often, inertia exerts its insidious influence much more slowly. It creeps in and takes root over a long period of time. No decision points clearly highlight inflections along the path. Inertia can manifest with great stealth.

It appears completely innocuous to the victim. Day in and day out nothing changes, and a foolish consistency emerges. The thoughts and decisions of one day are the same as the last, and then the next day, and the next, and so on. Once entrenched, these inertial thoughts resist change with all their might. Objects at rest tend to stay at rest.

The newspaper industry in the United States is the quintessential example of this type of stagnant and conventional thinking. Before the internet boom in the mid-1990s, newspapers profited handsomely by selling papers at a significant margin and raked in gobs of revenue from businesses buying traditional ad blocks and individuals placing classifieds ads. Business boomed, but then, with the explosion of the internet, began the decline.

Over the next two decades, newspaper revenues crashed and profits shriveled. Free content available via the internet undermined the paid subscription business model and readers migrated online in droves. With lower newspaper readership, traditional advertisers took their budgets elsewhere. Online marketplaces like Craigslist and eBay made it possible for individuals to sell their wares more cheaply and reach a broader audience than via traditional classified adverting. With just a small fraction of its historical readership and dwindling advertising revenue, the industry may never recover.

Yet, in the early 1990s, no company or industry stood better positioned than newspapers to win in the new era. All the journalists worked for newspapers giving the industry access to the biggest and best source of written content. Newspapers had established brands and fiercely loyal readership.

The industry also benefited from a remarkable history of cooperation. Established in 1846, the Associated Press enabled all contributing member newspapers access to each other's written material – a level of cooperation rarely seen in competitive marketplaces.

At the beginning of their decline, newspapers had all the advantages – the content providers, loyal readers, great brands, and cooperative competition. Flush with cash, they could have invested in the new technology. Journalists already on the payroll could have churned out superior content to devoted readership.

Before Craigslist could steal all the classified advertising revenue, a cooperative model like the AP could have inoculated the industry. The newspaper industry had all the customers who placed classifieds already. They could have launched their own Craigslist-type online classifieds. Competing newspapers could have formed an alliance to offer a national classified offering. It wouldn't have been unprecedented.

But the industry decided to wait. They decided to continue down the same path. Instead of embracing the inevitable, they delayed the launch and support of online editions. They never directly confronted the threats that drained the once rich adverting revenue streams dry. As a result, the industry now teeters on the verge of collapse. With the benefit of hindsight, one can clearly see the industry's mistake of failing to quickly respond to the internet threat.

But from the vantage point of the newspaper executive in the early 1990s, the threat didn't appear quite as obvious. Newspapers cycled through high and low periods several times before. Executives had grown accustomed to sales waxing and waning through peaks and troughs.

The industry had already flourished despite one potentially disruptive technology – the invention of television. Following the introduction of television in the 1950s, US newspaper advertising revenue grew an impressive $10 billion per decade.

The newspaper executive in the 1990s had experienced it all before — plenty of business cycles and unprecedented success despite the introduction and diffusion of television. They had seen it before. They had survived it before. They had thrived through it before. That was consistent for the entire past. Why would the future be any different?

Executives foolishly assumed that the future would resemble the past. They thoughtlessly expected they would survive in the rapidly evolving landscape without making meaningful strategic changes themselves.

At first, the declines were small. Executives dismissed them, ascribing the losses as minor leakage to a pesky upstart — no big deal.

Then the declines grew. But those moderate losses could be attributed to the economic downturn. Surely, profits would revert to higher levels the way they had in the past. They did before.

But this time they didn't. The landscape continued to shift. Eventually, the losses grew too large to ignore. But, by then, it was too late.

Over the course of the long decline, executives didn't face a single decision point where they had to choose between cleaving to the past and embracing the future. Even in the case of this relatively rapid collapse, the inevitable end snuck up on the newspaper industry slowly, over the course of two decades.

The industry didn't collapse because of a single bad decision. It failed because a group of leaders woke up every day for decades and plodded dutifully through their day. Every day, consistently, they did what they did the day before, without much new and independent thought. The mental effort they expended focused on rationalizing why the past cycles would repeat and performance would revert to historical means. They failed to place enough thought, and certainly not enough action, on the future and what it would take to win in the next decade.

Emerson calls this foolish consistency of doing the same thing every day without questioning the "hobgoblins of little minds." They just sort of creep in, slowly, over time, when people don't take the initiative to think differently or have the courage to change their mind given new circumstances. People fail to overcome their ingrained compulsion to believe the future will be like the past. Inertia compels them to remain consistent with past decisions, to not challenge conventional thinking, to not act courageously and change one's mind. Thoughts at rest tend to stay at rest.

Once these hobgoblins creep in, they prove hard to root out. And, as it turns out, newspapers have surrendered to foolish consistency for much longer than the last two decades. They have been doing it for centuries.

Vestigial Broadsheet

Did you ever wonder why newspapers are printed on such large unusually and inconveniently large sheets of paper? As it turns out, it wasn't always the case. Up until about 300 years ago, newspapers published their content on much smaller and more manageable sheets of paper.

It all changed in 1712. To increase tax revenue and better control news reporting, the British government passed the Stamp Act of 1712. The Act created a new tax on all publishers including newspapers. The British authorities levied the tax based on the number of pages in a publication. For newspapers, publishers had to pay a tax of one penny for each whole sheet of printed paper.

Newspapers faced a choice and they responded in a logical way. Since every page would be taxed one penny, they increased paper size to reduce total page count. Making this adjustment significantly reduced their total tax liability. These larger paper formats became known as broadsheets. Not surprisingly, the practice of printing on broadsheet quickly spread throughout the entire British Empire including the colonies.

To this day, the most popular newspapers in the world still publish in a broadsheet format. The most reputable and popular US newspapers including *The New York Times*, *The Washington Post*, and the *Wall Street Journal* publish in broadsheet. The most popular newspapers in the world including Japan's *Yomiuri Shimbun* and *Asahi Shimbun* and India's *The Times of India* publish in broadsheet. Millions and millions of readers all across the globe suffer through the inconvenience of trying to open, fold, and read on unwieldy pages.

At first, newspapers made a shift for the logical reason of tax avoidance, but that reason no longer exists. The

British government repealed The Stamp Act in 1855. Despite that, the newspaper industry has continued to print on the broadsheet unnecessarily for over 150 years.

Moreover, many of the largest circulation newspapers in the world never fell under the jurisdiction of the British Empire. And many weren't founded until after the Act was repealed: *Yomiuri Shimbun* (1874), *Asahi Shimbun* (1879), *Wall Street Journal* (1889), and *The Washington Post* (1877).

Newspapers had many great opportunities to transition away from broadsheet to a more convenient option. Papers could have changed when they moved into new markets with no established readership or limiting tax laws. Numerous technological changes also created opportunities for publishers to make the change.

Printing presses upgraded from wood to cast iron through the 1800s. Richard Hoe invented the rotary printing press in 1843 enabling large scale printing. In 1865, William Bullock invented the continuous roll process that enabled self-feeding greatly increasing capacity. In the late 19th and early 20th centuries, new Linotype machines enabled operators to typeset text a full line at a time instead of hand composing letter-by-letter. In the last few decades, computers revolutionized the entire printing process.

At every one of these inflection points, publishers invested in new technology. Each time, they had a fantastic opportunity to change publishing formats to improve the reader's experience by jettisoning broadsheet in favor of a smaller page. But they didn't.

A tax change forced newspapers to change to broadsheet over 300 years ago, but without a clear current purpose, broadsheet maintains its presence like a vestigial organ. It used to serve a purpose. It no longer does. Yet still it remains. A foolish consistency, a mental inertia, this is the hobgoblin of little minds.

Somewhere in Tokyo or New York, a commuter rides a subway to work and struggles to flip through the cumbersome pages. He gets frustrated. He tosses the paper to the side and decides to read the news on his smartphone.

CHAPTER 7

MAGINOT

"Generals always fight the last war, especially if they won it."

– Military Adage

Inertia exerts its ubiquitous influence in a wide array of situations. NBA players make quick decisions based on the outcome of a recent shot, momentum urging them in the direction of the trend – objects in motion. Newspaper executives unwittingly slip into a foolish consistency failing to ever take action – objects at rest. In both cases, players and executives make decisions in the moment. Either they decide to take a shot or they mindlessly resign to consistency each and every day.

Another type of decision-making provides fertile ground for mental inertia to take root.

Inertia flourishes when people or groups contemplate future actions. In these situations, when people have sufficient time to vet alternatives, inertia bends thinking toward the past.

Often, the larger and more important the decision, the stronger inertia's gravitational pull grows.

In these instances, people make careful choices. They evaluate alternatives, meticulously scrutinizing their options. They don't make decisions in the moment – they plan them conscientiously. Yet, inertia exerts its influence without prejudice. It anchors thinking, pulling and dragging thoughts backward. It compels people to think that the future will resemble the past.

The old military adage that Generals always fight the last war, especially if they won, typifies this type of inertia. And no anecdote epitomizes this maxim more than the story of France's construction of the Maginot Line.

In World War I Germany attacked France through Belgium. Starting in August 1914, the German Army made quick and terribly violent progress through neutral Belgium. By the end of August, the Germans already captured some strategic industrial areas of France. By September 1914, the German Army advanced within just 43 miles of Paris. Then, in the First Battle of the Marne, British and French troops thwarted the Germans' rapid advance, forcing them to retreat. Following the setback, the Germans pulled back slightly and established a trench position, British and French forces countered with trenches of their own establishing a fixed Western Front that would stand for the next three years.

The protracted trench warfare proved costly for both sides. Troops in uncomfortable trenches alternated between boredom and bombardment. For years, opposing armies pummeled each other with machine gun fire, artillery shells, and chlorine gas.

While the enemies traded attacks along the line, they each raced to outflank the other by building progressively longer trenches. Eventually, the trench system would stretch all the way to the North Sea coast in Belgium. For the remainder of the war, both sides poured substantial resources into extending, fortifying, and supplying the expanding line along the Western Front.

For the Germans, the extended trench along the Western front proved a costly stalemate for three years. They could never fully breach the barrier, reach Paris, and wrestle control of France. For the French and The Allies, the stalemate proved successful in holding the German attackers at bay, their advance stalled and controlled.

Although extremely costly in human lives, protracted trench warfare ultimately proved effective for France. They suffered losses, but defended their sovereignty, and with the help of reinforcements from other Allied Powers, eventually prevailed in WWI. In the end, the static defensive posture stalemated Germany eventually enabling an Allied victory.

With the anguish of WWI still fresh in their minds, France debated how to respond to future attacks. The debates took place over several years. Leaders on both sides of the argument agreed that France needed to prepare for war, but they disagreed greatly on strategy.

Several prominent politicians and military leaders including Charles de Gaulle favored an aggressive posture. Proponents of this strategy recommended investments in tanks and aircraft. They argued that France would need advanced weaponry to win a future war with an enemy who would have made technological advances of their own.

Others believed France should assume a more defensive stance. Marshal Joffre, the General who led the French to victory at the First Battle of the Marne, proposed an extensive defensive fortification system. Joffre and other proponents of this strategy argued that a well-defended barrier would prove effective in stopping a German ground advance and save millions of French lives.

During the 1930 budget debate, another WWI veteran, French Minister of War André Maginot, took the lead and argued that France should pursue defensive fortifications. The strategy would require underfunding the other more aggressive parts of the French Military, but that didn't matter.

France was convinced that Germany would attack as they did decades earlier. The trench had stopped the German's advance before. And, with the benefit of time to prepare, France could build an even better system of defensive fortifications.

Maginot argued convincingly and garnered overwhelming support in Parliament's Upper House, winning the vote 274-26. By the end of the debates, Maginot convinced Parliament to invest 3.3 Billion Francs to construct an elaborate and extensive fortification system facing the border with Germany.

France made its choice. They would defend.

From 1930-1940, France poured prodigious resources into construction of the defensive fortification system known as the Maginot line. But it was much more than a "line." It was a state-of-the-art, multilayer defensive machine that extended 16 miles deep in places.

The outer layers of the "line" contained early warning stations, but further inward the defenses grew more substantial. Antitank rails sprouted uninterrupted for hundreds of miles to stalemate the progress of German tanks. Well-stocked bunkhouses of various purposes peppered the countryside surrounding the line. Complex bunker systems known as "overages" housed France's heaviest artillery and between 500-1,000 men. In total, there were 142 overages, all connected via a system of underground electric railways and tunnels. Each overage had an independent ventilation system, barracks, water storage, food storage, and cafeteria.

The forward line included 5,000 "blockhouses" to house infantry armed with anti-tank and anti-personnel weaponry. The line also included 352 infantry casements equipped with twin-machine guns and anti-tank artillery. France strategically placed over 1,000 steel and concrete structures known as cloches along the line. The bell-shaped turrets protruded just enough from the ground to allow French infantry to target the enemy, but not to expose themselves to enemy fire.

The French also constructed shelters for reserve troops, ammunition depots, and electric transmission systems. They laid heavy rail support lines to transport tanks and fabricated large basins that could be flooded on command to slow the enemy's progress.

In total, the line spanned 943 miles stretching from the Swiss Alps to the English Channel. The 280-mile section along the Franco-German boarder extended from Luxembourg to Switzerland and contained the most substantial defenses.

When fully constructed, French Military experts considered the line a masterwork of genius, completely impervious to a direct attack. The military and the citizenry of France rested well, confident that they had made the necessary preparations. It took a decade to construct and cost billions of Francs. But if Germany attacked, just like they did in WWI, France would be ready.

In spring of 1940, the Germans staged their attack. Initially, they set up a small decoy force in direct opposition to the Maginot line. Meanwhile, they deftly readied a larger force to the North, near Belgium. Then, on March 10, 1940, they attacked.

Unlike the slow plodding attacks that characterized WWI, the Germans changed their tactics. They moved quickly. They acted decisively. Instead of lumbering headlong into the impenetrable line, the Germans deftly outflanked the French to the North. They swiftly attacked through the Ardennes forest. In just a few days, the Germans sent over one million men and 1,500 tanks through a forest that the French thought impenetrable.

While the German infantry completely bypassed the most formidable portion of the line, the German Luftwaffe simply flew over it. France was quickly overwhelmed. It took the Germans only five days to penetrate France through the Ardennes. And it took the Germans just five weeks to accomplish what they failed to do in WWI. On June 14, 1940, Germany took control of Paris. One week later, on June 22nd, just six weeks following the start of the attack, France fell. In just 43 days, Germany completely conquered France.

France prepared to fight the same static trench war that they did in WWI. But Germany changed their tactics. Germany employed Blitzkrieg and attacked with speed and surprise. They moved quickly, going around on the ground and over in the air. The French generals fought the last war, and it cost them greatly.

Mental inertia exerts an insidious and pervasive influence on decision making. Already predisposed to consistency, people easily succumb to its ensnaring effect. Momentum bends thinking in the direction of the trend. Consistency creeps in, and over time, its grooves cut deeper making thought and behavior patterns more difficult to change. Prisoners to precedent, people make decisions by planning for the past, not the future.

But the past doesn't perfectly predict the future. A made shot doesn't mean you should shoot more. The business cycles of the past won't repeat indefinitely. New threats won't always be dispatched the same way as old ones. A decision to increase paper size doesn't need to endure beyond the law it helped to circumvent. New wars aren't always fought like old wars.

With perspective, these truths seem obvious. But, perhaps, it's no more obvious than the color of the squares on Adelson's checkerboard. Humans easily make these mistakes. The best players and the smartest executives share the same shortcomings. Generals with their own lives, the lives of millions of countrymen, and their nation's sovereignty at risk fall into the same traps. Inertia wields an incredibly strong and omnipresent drag on decision making.

But, despite its powerful influence, people possess the ability to overcome the mental inertia that binds them to the metaphorical shoal. One can break free and zag! However, as these next few examples will show, zagging requires one to think differently and recognize the opportunity in an alternative approach and then to make the difficult choice to act differently and break from the shoal.

CHAPTER 8

PAST PERFORMANCE

"The future ain't what it used to be."

– Yogi Berra

In 1924, Massachusetts Investors Trust pioneered a concept that would grow into a behemoth industry with assets exceeding the size of the entire United States economy.* Its innovation created the first true open ended "mutual fund" which enabled individual investors to easily pool their money for investment purposes. More importantly, it allowed investors to continuously purchase additional shares and redeem them without having to dissolve the entire investment company. By the end of its first year of operations, the Massachusetts Investors Trust had 200 shareholders and $392,000 in assets.

From these humble beginnings, a colossal industry blossomed. By the end of 2015, worldwide net mutual fund assets totaled over $37 trillion dollars with United States registered investment companies alone managing over $18

---

* Per ICI 2016 Fact Book, 2015 net mutual fund assets totaled $37 trillion compared to the US economy which was $17.9 trillion in 2015.

trillion in assets. In the United States, an estimated 54.9 million households owned mutual funds with over 90% investing in them to save for retirement.

Given the importance of retirement saving, one might expect that people would make wise and thoughtful choices when investing their nest eggs in mutual funds.

One would be wrong.

Since the advent of mutual funds until the present day, most investors focused on the past to guide their future investment decisions. As a result, many have made terrible choices about how to invest their hard-earned cash.

In the mid-1970s, the industry was still nascent in its development. By 1980, only 6% of US households invested in mutual funds. Then, buoyed by rising household incomes and an extended bull market, mutual fund ownership commenced a tremendous period of growth. By 1996, the number of households owning mutual funds had increased 8 times and the number of available funds had grown to a dizzying 18,572.

Investors faced a staggering number of investment choices. When asked which sources of information they reviewed prior to making investment decisions, investors responded as follows:[*]

- 75% considered Past Performance
- 69% Risk
- 49% Investment Goals

---

[*] Based on a 1996 survey conducted by the Investment Company Institute, a national association of US registered investment companies.

- 46% Portfolio Securities
- 43% Fees and Expenses.

Investors relied on "past performance" as the primary factor for determining which funds to buy. An overwhelming 75% used it to guide their decision making. And, digging deeper into how investors assess "Risk" suggests that past performance plays an even more crucial role.

When assessing "Risk," investors favored reviewing the history of past annual performance results. If the fund had stable returns in the past, investors expected stable returns in the future. If the fund generated highly variable returns, investors expected high variability in the future.

Prospective investors not only used past performance as their primary source of information, they also relied heavily on past performance to determine fund risk, the second most important factor informing investment decisions.

One can see the logic in the approach. Faced with a staggering array of choices, investors looked to an abundantly available, well-documented source of information about performance. Sounds reasonable, right?

Most people, including the majority of mutual fund investors thought so. And, at first blush, examining past history seems like a sensible way to evaluate prospective investments. But empirical evidence suggests that using past performance is an absolutely lousy way to predict future performance. Consider for a moment the following facts regarding mutual fund returns:

- Funds that outperform in any 3-year period are likely to underperform in the subsequent 3-year period.
- For the past five decades, the average performance of the top 20 funds in a given decade underperformed the market average in the next decade.*

Strong performance today does not lead to strong performance tomorrow. In fact, the opposite appears to be true.

So, if past performance does not guarantee future returns, why do investors look to the past when it clearly doesn't lead to good decisions? Why, despite sufficient evidence to the contrary, do investors continue to rely on the past to predict the future?

Because mental inertia is a powerful and persistent force that often masquerades as common sense. Newton's First Law of Motion applied to cognitive processes provides a compelling answer. Translating Newton's First Law to investing decisions: Overperforming funds will continue to overperform, and underperforming funds will continue to underperform.

Mental inertia hardwired into the minds of investors drives them to believe that strong past performance will lead to strong future performance. They comb through the financial pages looking to the past and spend money on financial magazines and investment services that document

---

* Using United States equity fund data from 1985-2005.

the top performing funds of the past year and past decades. Investors seek out the "hot" fund managers who lead very successful funds and shift their money accordingly.

These investors wholeheartedly believe that are making well-informed and prudent investment decisions that will ultimately prove successful. In reality, they have succumbed to mental inertia which has ensnared them resulting in bad choices.

Against this current of conventional wisdom, one man decided to swim upstream. He had a novel idea. He observed that past mutual fund performance didn't predict the future. He also observed that fund managers spend incredibly large amounts of money researching and trading stocks in their funds to try and maximize performance.

So, he conducted a detailed study that compared the performance of actively managed mutual funds to the S&P 500 stock market index.* What he discovered would revolutionize the mutual fund industry.

John Bogle's study showed that 75% of mutual funds failed to beat the performance of the S&P 500 index. He learned that fund managers actually picked stocks that performed about as well as the S&P 500. But the fund managers incurred such large research and trading expenses that their overall performance lagged the Index. In addition to the excessive costs, all of their active trading created much higher tax liability for investors. After he accounted

---

* The S&P 500 is a stock market index that is based on 500 large US companies. Its performance is dependent on the 500 companies that comprise the index. It is considered one of the better ways of measuring performance of the US equity market.

for all the costs, Bogle revealed the surprising truth. Most investors could make more money if they could just invest in the S&P 500 than if they invested in a traditional mutual fund.

Based on this insight, Bogle created a new type of fund. While other funds were "actively" managed racking up excessive costs in an attempt to outperform each other and the market index, Bogle designed his fund to simply match the S&P 500's performance. This "passive" management style resulted in significantly lower costs. He named his new fund the Vanguard 500 Index Fund.

The fund simply bought the individual stocks included in the S&P 500 Index in the proportion in which they comprised the Index. As a result, his fund required limited oversight and incurred relatively low transaction costs. The simple strategy resulted in very predictable returns – yields that were virtually identical to those of the S&P every single year.

Since the majority of funds fail to beat the S&P Index and the ones that do outperform in a given time period are likely to underperform in the next period, Bogle's fund became an outstanding success. In just a few decades, starting from just a single fund, Vanguard has grown into the world's second largest mutual fund company. In September 2014, Vanguard surpassed $3 trillion in assets under management equaling the size of the entire hedge fund industry. Today, Vanguard manages over $3.4 trillion in assets spread over 300 funds.

Bogle ignored the conventional thinking that past performance would predict future results and realized that despite an individual fund manager's best efforts, they consistently failed to outperform the market average.

Bogle made the choice to zag. He created a new type of mutual fund that propelled his company to greatness and revolutionized an entire industry.

CHAPTER 9

SHIFT

"There is nothing new to be discovered in physics now. All that remains is more and more precise measurement."

– Lord Kelvin

Inertia skews mutual fund investor's sights to the past, compelling them to make poor decisions with their hard-earned money. To revolutionize the industry, Bogle had to identify and commercialize an entirely new approach. But to realize the opportunity in an alternative approach, one must change the way he or she views and interprets the world around them. They must shift their own thinking. The world doesn't change, but the way that one perceives and comprehends it does.

Thomas Kuhn coined the phrase "Paradigm Shift" in the early 1960s to describe step-change leaps forward that create a radical change in belief. In Kuhn's original explanation, he used the now-famous duck-rabbit illusion to demonstrate his point. In the following illusion, one sees either a duck or a rabbit depending on perspective.

The picture doesn't change, but the way that one views and interprets the image does. Kuhn used this construct to explain the outcomes of scientific revolution. According to Kuhn, after a revolution, the entire worldview of the scientific community changes. While the physical realities of the world remain the same, the way the community thinks about and understands the world shifts dramatically. Where once one saw only a duck, one shifts their perspective to see a rabbit.

Due to mental inertia, people tend to remain anchored in their current worldview until they break free and put on new lenses, shift their perspective, and view the world differently. But people's existing worldviews are not as easily malleable as shifting from duck to rabbit. Worldviews are forged by a lifetime of experiences, becoming deeply ingrained into the fabric of one's being.

Changing the way, the world thinks requires not only a brilliant recognition of an alternative worldview, but determination, conviction, and persistence to stay the course, shift the paradigm, and zag.

Gedanken Experiments

Just five years after Lord Kelvin made his infamous proclamation that there was nothing new to discover in Physics, Albert Einstein published his paper on Special Relativity. Einstein's new way to understand and explain the world would eventually transform Physics and overthrow the incumbent thinking which had governed the field for over two hundred years. However, the paradigm shift wouldn't occur immediately.

Prior to Einstein, Newtonian or Classical mechanics dominated thinking in the field of Physics. For the most part, classical mechanics worked well in explaining what scientists observed in the real world. But some limitations of classical mechanics perplexed physicists of the day.

Oversimplifying for the sake of brevity, the limitations included explaining the behavior of very small and very quickly moving objects, understanding the nature and behavior of light, and reconciling confounding issues regarding the interrelation between space, time, and gravity.

To address the unresolved issues, most physicists of the day focused on experimentation and equation solving. They attempted to distill truth by designing increasingly sophisticated and complex experiments to better measure natural phenomena and by developing increasingly complex equations to explain their observations.

More measurement, better measurement. More equations, better equations. This was the conventional approach taken by the majority of physicists.

However, a little-known patent clerk from Bern, Switzerland did not subscribe to this conventional approach. Einstein engaged in Gedanken or "thought experiments" to devise his famous theories.*

In contemplating the behavior of light, Einstein didn't try to measure its speed or triangulate equations to find truth. Instead, he imagined what it would be like to ride alongside a beam of light. In an attempt to better understand space and time and gravity, Einstein imagined people riding on trains, elevators, or standing still. He contemplated how they would observe phenomenon such as a lightning strike based on their relative positions and velocities.

Einstein used these thought experiments to develop his Theory of Relativity. In his 1905 paper, *Special Relativity*, Einstein postulated that all motion or rest is in relation to other objects and that light always moved at a constant speed.

Today, these assertions appear rather benign. But the implications from these rather straightforward postulates in the early 1900s were staggering. Einstein demonstrated that time between two events could not be absolute, but would be dependent on the reference frame or velocity of the people observing the events. This proved that time doesn't pass at the same rate for everyone. It depends on the speed at which one is traveling. If Special Relativity were true, time

---

* Einstein did eventually use some rather sophisticated mathematics to describe the theories he developed using thought experiments. However, and contrary to popular belief, Einstein was a relatively average mathematician when compared to the other leading Physicists of his era.

and space could no longer be considered absolute or even independent constructs. Shocking revelations!*

A couple years later in 1907, back in the Bern patent office, Einstein conducted another famous thought experiment which led to a revelation he later described as "the happiest thought of my life." Einstein heard a story about a house painter who fell off a roof while painting. The house painter recounted that he didn't feel anything negative while he was falling. He only felt pain when he hit the ground.

To the average person, this would be nothing more than a sad story about an unfortunate housepainter. To Einstein, this was divine inspiration that proved gravity and acceleration must be equivalent. Newton had his Apple. Einstein had his housepainter. This insight led to nearly a decade of work focused on expanding Special Relativity into a more generalized theory that unified space, time, and gravity. The result was Einstein's masterwork: General Relativity.

Einstein used thought experiments to push classical mechanics to its breaking point. While his contemporaries spent their time in the lab scribbling out equation after equation on the chalkboard, Einstein spent the majority of his time in thought. His innovative approach helped him break from the shackles of mental inertia, shift his thinking, and develop transcendental theories.

Newton zagged when he developed and wrote *Principles* laying the foundation for Classical mechanics. Over two

---

* Special Relativity also gave birth to the now famous equation: $e = mc2$ which describes the relationship between mass and energy.

centuries later, Newton's thinking was no longer revolutionary. It had become conventional and its limitations had become apparent. Then Einstein came along and started another revolution in thought. Like Newton before him, Einstein eschewed the conventional thinking of the day and chose to think differently than centuries of scientists who came before him. Einstein overcame mental inertia and zagged. As a result, Einstein achieved remarkable success and acclaim.

The leaps forward made by Einstein are exactly the types of scientific revolutions that define the classic "Paradigm Shift." While the physical realities of the world don't change, the way the scientific community thinks about and understands the world does. At one point, the scientific community only saw a rabbit, but the great scientific revolutionaries, through sheer brilliance, protracted effort, and personal sacrifice, helped the world eventually see the duck.

CHAPTER 10

A NEW MODEL(S)

"Most companies that are great at something - like AOL dialup or Borders bookstores - do not become great at new things people want (streaming for us) because they are afraid to hurt their initial business."

– Reed Hastings, co-founder and CEO of Netflix

In 1997, Reed Hastings rented a copy of *Apollo 13* from his local Blockbuster video store. Like countless others before him, he misplaced the video cassette and didn't return it to the store early enough to avoid a late fee. By the time, he returned the tape, he had racked up a $40 charge. Frustrated by the situation and inspired by a trip to his local gym, Reed Hastings had an idea that would revolutionize the video rental industry.

Before Hastings revolutionized the industry, there were nearly 25,000 video rental stores in the United States operated by major corporations such as Blockbuster and thousands of smaller independent companies. They all functioned with essentially the same business model. Customers visited a physical store location, rented a movie or video game for a short time, and then came back to the store to return the rental. If customers didn't return the rental in time, they were charged a fine known as a "late fee."

Hastings observed that gyms employ a completely different business model. Gyms charge a flat, usually monthly, membership fee and then allow members to use the gym as little or as much as they would like. Hastings reasoned that eliminating late fees and offering unrestricted usage might be a better model for the video rental industry.

Hastings had a great insight, but he still had a choice to make. He could open a new chain of video rental stores, similar in nearly every way to the established market, except for a different, flat-rate pricing structure. Or, he could use the insight as inspiration, and go further and launch an entirely new model with potential to revolutionize the industry.

He chose the latter. In 1998, Hastings founded Netflix.

His new business model required no retail stores. Rather, customers would request movies online and then Netflix would mail the movies using the US postal service. Members paid a flat monthly fee with no late charges, and could rent as many movies as they wanted in a month. Because Netflix wasn't limited by space restrictions, they could offer an assortment of movies that dwarfed the selection available in a traditional video-rental store. And, perhaps even more importantly, Netflix videos were always available unlike in traditional stores that were plagued with out-of-stocks leading to frustrated customers.

About two years after Hastings launched Netflix, the reigning industry behemoth Blockbuster had an opportunity to purchase the still fledgling Netflix for a mere $50 million.

Blockbuster refused. And Blockbuster would pay a heavy price.

Blockbuster eventually offered its customers a flat membership rate pricing structure, and, after much delay, created their own mail-order operation. But it was too little, too late for the struggling incumbent and the rest of the industry establishment.

Netflix quickly ate into the sales of traditional video stores and their profits plummeted.

In 2004, Blockbuster had 60,000 employees and over 9,000 stores. By 2010, it had filed for Chapter 11 bankruptcy protection. Over that same time, Netflix exploded. By 2009, Netflix offered a collection of over 100,000 DVDs and surpassed the 10 million subscriber mark. Shortly after the ink was dry on Blockbuster's Chapter 11 paperwork, in April 2011, Netflix reached 23 million subscribers in the US and 26 million worldwide.

The new Netflix model completely disrupted the industry and overthrew the establishment. In less than a decade, Blockbuster was dead and Netflix was king. But Netflix's position on the throne was far from secure.

Netflix was flying high in the spring of 2011. Membership continued to grow in the wake of the traditional video rental market collapse. The stock price was at a record high and Netflix was a Wall Street darling. But technology was about to change everything.

Rapid increases in video streaming capability enabled by increased computing speed and internet bandwidth expansion made video on demand viable for the first time. Instead of renting a DVD either from a store or through the mail, consumers could get content delivered directly to their home via the internet. Less than a decade after mail-order DVDs usurped the incumbent store rental business, streaming video threatened to obsolete the mail-order model. Netflix's legacy business was under attack.

But, unlike Blockbuster, Netflix didn't bind itself to the past. Netflix embraced the future. Netflix made a few early mistakes. Initially, they contemplated launching a separate streaming service with a new brand name and website. The stock price tumbled, but Netflix quickly reconsidered and adjusted. Netflix acted flexibly and nimbly in not only deciding to pursue streaming, but in adjusting their commercialization approach.

Whereas Blockbuster cleaved to the past model, Netflix unshackled itself and moved forward creating a new model vastly superior to its old one.

Blockbuster was afraid to hurt its initial business. They were mired in the past and died as a result. Netflix reinvented itself and thrived.

In the new streaming market, Netflix continues to innovate and stay at the forefront of change. The company has traveled beyond merely distributing video content to actually producing video content. Netflix has already created and developed scores of Netflix-exclusive shows including award winning programs such as *House of Cards* and *Orange is the New Black*.

By 2015, Netflix subscriber count surpassed 65 million including over 23 million international subscribers. In the US, during peak evening hours, Netflix consumed roughly one-third of America's internet capacity. Today, Netflix's stock trades at or near an all-time high.

Hastings and Netflix zagged twice. First, they disrupted an entire industry. Then, just a decade later, they did it again. They overcame the inertial forces that led to the demise of many former industry leaders like Blockbuster. But perhaps more importantly, Hastings built a nimble company unafraid to obsolete itself and seemingly immune from inertia.

Undoubtedly, there will be another technology shift that disrupts the video industry – and it will be fun to watch and see if Netflix can zag again.

CHAPTER 11

FINDING LONGITUDE

"The Discovery of the Longitude is of such Consequence to Great Britain for the safety of the Navy and Merchant Ships as well as for the improvement of Trade that for want thereof many Ships have been retarded in their voyages, and many lost."

– Longitude Act of 1714

In late October 1707, Commander-in-Chief of the British Fleets, Sir Cloudesley Shovell led a fleet of 21 ships on a voyage back home to Britain. The ships had recently been involved in a battle in the Mediterranean during the War of the Spanish Succession. Terrible weather and persistent squalls made the return trip incredibly difficult even for the veteran commander and experienced crew. Over the lengthy journey, storms gradually pushed the fleet off its planned course.

On the night of October 22nd, the crew thought they were approaching the final leg of their voyage. But they were tragically mistaken. Before they realized their mistake, several of the ships slammed into the rocks just off the Isles of Scilly. Instead of smoothly sailing home, 1,550 sailors died when their ships slammed into the rocky archipelago at the southwestern corner of Great Britain.

Because of adverse weather conditions, the ships navigators had no way to accurately calculate their position in the open sea. They couldn't "find longitude."

At the time, navigators employed a technique known as dead-reckoning to calculate their position at sea. The process requires a navigator to first identify a specific point with a known location then carefully measure the angle and speed of travel from that point. In practice, a navigator might know that his ship sailed past a certain island at 8AM then traveled at 10 knots toward the south until 9AM. Knowing the starting point, the speed, and direction would allow the navigator to approximate his location in the open sea.

Under ideal conditions, the method worked reasonably well. However, the method proved terribly inaccurate when weather conditions made it nearly impossible to know a ship's exact trajectory and speed. Small mistakes in the calculations compounded the longer a ship spent in the open sea without encountering a known point to re-calibrate the reckoning.

As transoceanic travel grew more common, the need for reliable open sea navigation became increasingly critical. And, in the wake of the maritime disaster that cost 1,550 sailors their lives, the demand for something better than dead-reckoning became an urgent priority.

In 1714, the Parliament of Great Britain took action and passed the Longitude Act. The Act established a series of monetary awards for anyone who could determine a way to "find longitude" at sea and provided higher monetary rewards based on level of accuracy. The Act also established the Board of Longitude – a government body charged with administering the prizes and encouraging the best innovators in the world to focus on the problem of "finding longitude" at sea.

The prizes were large – the equivalent of several million of today's dollars. The stakes were high – lives were on the line. The profile was elevated – the Act and the efforts were supported by the Queen of England.

But the challenge was immense. Many used the expression "finding longitude" to mean "doing the impossible." The leading thinkers and scientists considered "finding longitude" the greatest scientific challenge of the times.

In theory, finding longitude was a rather simple concept. For every 15 degrees that one travels eastward, the local time moves exactly one hour ahead. Conversely, for every 15 degrees that one travels westward, the local time moves one hour backward. So, to calculate the exact longitude at any point on Earth, a navigator in the 1700s only needed to know two things. They need to know the exact time in their current location and the exact time at some known place on Earth such as the Prime Meridian in Greenwich. From there, the navigator could cross-reference those two times in a navigational chart to determine their precise longitude.

While simple in theory, finding longitude proved extremely difficult in practice. Navigators could easily calculate the correct local time by observing the position of the sun, but knowing the exact time in Greenwich posed a vexing challenge.

Many of brightest minds in the world, including luminaries such as Isaac Newton, began to contemplate the problem. And virtually all of the leading thinkers of the time, including Newton, favored essentially the same approach. Conventional wisdom held that one could only accurately know the reference time in Greenwich by employing a process known as the Lunar Distance method.

Proponents of this approach reasoned that the motion of the moon and the stars could act as a natural clock. If seafaring navigators could accurately measure the moon's position relative to known stars, they could compare those observations to carefully constructed tables that detailed the moon's position at every time of the day. By cross-referencing this "lunar almanac," navigators could identify the time in Greenwich. If they had the time in Greenwich and the local time based on the sun's position, they could know their precise longitude.

But the lunar distance method had many problems. If the sky was cloudy, navigators wouldn't be able to see the moon. Even if the moon could be seen, a very precise measurement of its location was challenging. Additionally, even with smooth seas, the "lunar almanac" table had several measurement errors.

Because of these challenges, many considered "finding longitude" a fool's errand. The brightest innovators of the time thought that if mankind were to ever solve this near-impossible task, there was only one way that could work – the lunar distance method.

One man thought differently. He thought differently than all the greatest minds of his time, including Newton. John Harrison zagged.

Instead of attempting to deduce the time in Greenwich through lunar observation, he opted for a much more direct approach. He decided to build a clock.

To a modern reader, building a clock might seem like a blindingly obvious solution to knowing the time. But in the early 1700s, even the boldest thinkers would have considered building a clock that would accurately maintain the time in Greenwich for an extended ocean voyage an absolutely preposterous idea.

Isaac Newton, perhaps the greatest thinker to ever walk the planet, thought the idea ludicrous and believed it impossible. Newton offered this scathing criticism of Harrison's preferred approach: "a good watch may serve to keep a reckoning at sea for some days and to know the time of a celestial observation.... But when longitude at sea is lost, it cannot be found again by any watch."

John Harrison's plan was simple in theory. Navigators could accurately calculate the local time using the position of the sun and they could know the exact time in Greenwich using a new clock that he would build. Navigators could then cross reference those two times in a very simple table to find their exact longitude.

Experienced navigators would have no problem reckoning local time. The approach required no math. And it would work with cloudy skies or rocky seas. It was an elegant solution. He just had to build a clock that would work. And that would be the hard part.

Harrison's clock would have to be unaffected by temperature and impervious to humidity. It would have to be non-corrosive despite prolonged exposure to salty air. It would have to work on a moving ship on turbulent seas. And it would have to remain accurate for a very long time.

Each individual obstacle presented a vexing problem that would require a major breakthrough to overcome. Taken together, the series of hurdles created a seemingly insurmountable challenge.

It would take decades and several iterations, but Harrison would eventually prevail. He took on each obstacle and conquered it with a novel solution and gritty determination.

Most clocks of Harrison's time employed a pendulum to measure time. But pendulums rely on a stable base to maintain accuracy. As a result, they all quickly lost time when aboard a moving boat. Even worse, they completely failed under turbulent conditions.

So, Harrison developed clocks that didn't require a pendulum – first with springs and later with balanced interconnected wheels. With the wheel-based approach, any motion that effected one wheel was perfectly offset on the other. Over the decades, Harrison continued to refine the design, eventually developing the caged roller bearing. This approach not only solved the problem of motion and turbulence, it enabled Harrison to dramatically decrease the size of the timepiece. Instead of requiring a massive-sea clock, the innovation, which is still employed today, allowed Harrison to build a highly accurate pocket watch that would keep accurate time through extreme turbulence.

Solving the problem of changing temperature, pressure and corrosion also required innovations. Fluctuating conditions either thickened or thinned the oil used to lubricate the clock's internal mechanisms. While others focused on developing better oils that would hold up under fluctuating conditions, Harrison designed clocks that didn't require any oil at all.

Even more importantly, Harrison invented the bi-metallic strip to address the problem created by changing temperature. In the strip, Harrison bound together two types of metal that expanded and contracted at different rates. In effect, he created a regulator that allowed the watch to function the same way regardless of ambient temperature.

After 31 years of work, Harrison completed what we know today as the Marine Chronometer – a portable watch that can accurately keep time on a transoceanic journey. Harrison's invention would revolutionize navigation and accelerate development of global trade and colonialism. In short, he changed the world.

Harrison zagged when he chose to pursue a different path than the establishment. He zagged when he developed novel solutions to longstanding watch making problems. And, as his story shows, sometimes even remarkable zaggers like Isaac Newton can act like sardines.

Post Script

Many forces bind our thinking and actions to the metaphorical shoal. The first one, the mental equivalent of Newton's First Law of Motion, is hardwired in the human mind and drives people to think and act conventionally. Mental inertia leads to pervasive belief that "the past predicts the future." People, ensnared by inertia, become committed to the past and act in accordance with that commitment. An object in motion tends to stay in motion.

Other victims of inertia fail to challenge conventional thinking and understanding about the world. They blindly and willingly accept that current beliefs and practices are correct, complete, and acceptable. And so, they simply accept the conventional wisdom and do nothing. An object at rest tends to stay at rest.

But one can overcome the powerful pull of mental inertia. By making a difficult and purposeful choice to think and act differently, many have zagged and achieved greatness. But unfortunately, inertia isn't the only powerful force which keeps people zigging along in the shoal…

Part Three

Risk

CHAPTER 12

PROTECT AND THRIVE

"There was only one catch and that was Catch-22, which specified that a concern for one's own safety in the face of dangers that were real and immediate was the process of a rational mind."

– *Catch-22* by Joseph Heller

Most believe the genesis of modern civilization occurred in approximately 10,000 BC in a lush region nestled between the Tigris and Euphrates Rivers in Mesopotamia. In Greek, Mesopotamia literally means "between rivers" and refers to the Tigris-Euphrates system which begins in Southern Turkey and extends through Syria and Iraq, eventually ending where the two rivers flow into the Persian Gulf.

Today, Mesopotamia mostly consists of hot and sandy dessert regions. However, in Neolithic times, water from the Tigris and Euphrates rivers nurtured a fertile ecosystem thriving with luxurious green fauna. Water and rich soil produced robust vegetation which, in turn, attracted an abundance of animals. The fruitfulness and productiveness of the area would also attract the ancestors of modern day humans.

Prior to settling in Mesopotamia, our ancestors sustained themselves largely through nomadic hunting and foraging. However, the area's bounty coupled with the development of irrigation techniques enabled our ancestors to transition to a more sedentary agrarian-based lifestyle.

In the Fertile Crescent, people no longer needed to travel constantly to sustain themselves. They could settle down, build homes, and thrive on the harvest of a single region. Single homes blossomed into villages which grew into small cities. In fertile Mesopotamia, civilization was born.

Prior to settling into a sedentary agrarian lifestyle, early humans derived sustenance by actively foraging for food and hunting wild animals. Procuring enough food to sustain life presented an ongoing and difficult daily challenge for the hunter-gatherers. This challenge necessitated a nomadic lifestyle putting tribes continually on the move looking for sustenance.

Some days brought feast and others famine depending on the ability to locate a good foraging location. When foraging proved too difficult, hunter-gatherers reluctantly resorted to the more dangerous pursuit of hunting with primitive weapons.

The ongoing quest for food dominated the hunter-gatherer's life – scavenging, gathering, and hunting, constantly going out, often in the face of great peril, attempting to procure enough food to sustain life.

Succeed and live. Fail and starve.

The life of a sedentary farmer differed greatly from that of a nomadic hunter-gatherer. And these differences would ultimately play a decisive role in establishing the way humans think and act in modern times.

In contrast to the nomadic hunting-gatherers, the quest for food did not dominate life for the sedentary farmer. Growing food enabled the farmers to build a calorie surplus. Certain foods, such as grains, enabled extended storage. With a surplus of food that could be stored for a long time, people in primitive communities could spend more time on other pursuits.

Because of the surplus, people could settle down and develop specialized skills. This specialization spurred economic growth, and in turn, the proliferation of civilization.

Instead of waking up and facing feast or famine depending on the success of the hunt, the sedentary agrarian communities needed to patiently and diligently tend to their crops and protect their surplus of food.

Grow and store. Protect and thrive.

Agrarian-based civilizations would blossom and spread across the entire globe. This economic model of specialization of labor predicated on creating and protecting a food surplus underpins today's modern societies as well. As a result, people living today, by virtue of both cultural heritage and contemporary demands face a situation similar in many ways to that of the early sedentary farmers. Unlike the hunter-gatherers who grew accustomed to dramatic swings between feast and famine, most living today have grown used to a predictable lifestyle predicated on accumulation and protection of food and other assets.

Grow and store. Protect and thrive.

Humans have slowly adapted to, and now desire, a life with little risk.

CHAPTER 13

DECISIONS, DECISIONS

"An investment said to have an 80% chance of success sounds far more attractive than one with a 20% chance of failure. The mind can't easily recognize that they are the same."

– Daniel Kahneman

We have evolved to have an aversion for risk. When our ancestors heard a rustle in the bushes, they feared a predator, acted accordingly, and survived to reproduce. Our ancestors also grew crops and protected the food surplus enabling our species to build great civilizations. As humans, our forbearers endowed us with a strong preference for safety, certainty, and security. Our genetic and cultural inheritance is to avoid risk and loathe loss.

But one can't completely avoid risk. Countless times, every day, people face choices and must make decisions under uncertainty. In these situations, shared cognitive biases bequeathed by our ancestors skew decisions in similar ways. As a result, people make predictable choices.

But mankind's relationship with risk is much more nuanced and complex than just trying to avoid risk at all cost. To better understand, let's take a look at a few possible choices to better understand our complicated relationship with risk:

In each of the following cases, chose A or B based on what you think is more desirable:

> Option A: You have an 80% chance of gaining $10,000 (and a 20% chance of gaining nothing).
>
> Option B: You have a 100% chance of gaining $7,000.

The expected value of Option A is higher ($8,000) than Option B ($7,000). A completely rational person making an entirely dispassionate and logical decision would chose A. But a majority of people select Option B, opting for the sure gain.

In this case, with high potential for a significant gain, people typically avoid risk. They typically make a **Risk Averse** selection.

> Option A: You have an 80% chance of losing $10,000 (and a 20% chance of losing nothing).
>
> Option B: You have a 100% chance of losing $7,000.

In this case, the expected value of choice B (loss of $7,000) is better than A (loss of $8,000). The rational choice is B. But this time a majority of people select Option A, opting for the chance to limit their losses.

Facing the prospect of a significant loss, most people don't take the sure thing and limit their losses. In these cases, people typically welcome risk in an effort to avoid the painful loss – they make a **Risk Seeking** selection.

The asymmetry of the choices illustrates an important bias in decision making. People hate "losing" more than they value "gaining." When faced with a gain, people will take the sure thing, but since people hate to lose so much, they are willing to take a risk to avoid the painful loss.

In other words, people feel greater pain from loss than they experience joy from an equivalent gain. To demonstrate, imagine that you find a $50 bill on the sidewalk. How happy would that make you feel? If you are like most, you would experience a moderate level of happiness. Now, imagine that you lost a $50 bill. How would that make you feel? If you are like the average person, you would experience a much greater level of pain.

To further delineate the point, imagine that you find a $50 bill and then lose it later in the day. At the end of the day, you would end up with $0, just like you started. But if you are like the average person, you will feel worse than if you never found the money in the first place.

Most people, making typical decisions, have a fairly similar and predictable relationship with gain, loss, and risk. Gains are good. They are to be protected and not risked.

But losses are terrible. They are to be avoided, even if avoiding them requires taking risk.

Gains are good. Risk is bad. Loss is the worst.

But our relationship with risk is even more nuanced. It's still predictable, but an interesting switch occurs when people encounter low probability choices.

To illustrate, let's take a look at another set of choices, but this time, we'll explore the tails of the probability curve:

Option A: Bet $1 on a 0.1% chance to win $900.

Option B: Do nothing.

In this case, the expected value of A is a loss of $0.10.* The economical choice would be to avoid making this bet. But, in the real world, we observe people frequently gambling and chose Option A. With low probability outcomes and high potential gains, people often display **Risk Seeking** behavior.

Option A: Take a 0.1% chance to lose $1,000,000.

Option B: Pay $1,100 to insure against that loss.

On average, Option A will result in a $1,000 loss making it the "economical" choice compared to Option B (a certain loss of $1,100). But when faced with a large potential loss,

---

* [($900 x $1 x 0.1%) - $1].

people typically favor **Risk Averse** behavior. They buy the insurance even if the expected value is a bit lower.

People are complex. The same people who act risk averse and buy insurance policies beyond their needs may also seek risk and buy lottery tickets. Sometimes we play it safe and take the sure gain, but sometimes we take irrational risks to avoid a loss. Our actions depend on the circumstances, but how people respond to various situations tends to be predictable.

Our collective genetic and cultural inheritance bequeaths us with similar biases that lead to similar actions under uncertainty. Sometimes we run from risk, and sometimes we run to it. But, collectively, we tend to travel in the same direction given similar circumstance. Our tendency to make similar choices leads to conventional behavior. To break free, one must exercise great strength to overcome this deeply ingrained relationship with risk.

CHAPTER 14

INSURANCE?

"There is a very easy way to return from a casino with a small fortune: go there with a large one."

– Jack Yelton

Blackjack, the most widely played casino table game in the world, offers an exceptional glimpse into humanity's complex relationship with risk.

The modern-day game of blackjack descends from an old French card game known as Vingt-et-un, or "Twenty-One." While casinos have made a few changes to the game over the years, the basic rules of the game remain the same.

Blackjack is a fairly simple game with relatively favorable odds when compared to many other casino games. Both factors contribute to the game's popularity.

In the most common version of the game, each player and the dealer draw an initial two card hand.* The player's cards are both visible to the players and the dealer, but one

---

* There are slight regional variants on the rules governing many aspects of the game. In the interest of simplicity and brevity, this game play explanation ignores many of these nuances.

of the dealer's cards is placed face-side downward such that only the dealer, and none of the players, can see.

After the initial two card deal, the players take turns drawing additional cards with the objective of attaining a hand value as close to 21 without going over. If a player exceeds 21, that player "busts" and loses his or her wager for that hand.

After the players' finish taking cards, the dealer starts to draw. The dealer begins by flipping over the previously unexposed card and tallying the total value of his hand. If the value of the hand is 17 or greater, the dealer will not take any additional cards. If the value is below 17, the dealer must continue to take additional cards until his total exceeds 17. If the dealer exceeds 21, then the dealer "busts" and every player who hasn't busted themselves will win their wager on that hand.

After the dealer is done taking cards, the final hand value of each player is compared to the hand value of the dealer. The players who have higher values than the dealer will win the value of their wager, and those with hand values below the dealers will lose their wager.

In the game, the best hand value a player can draw is a 21. If the player draws a 21 with their initial two card draw, that player has a "blackjack" and will get paid 1.5 times the amount they wagered. In order to draw a "blackjack," the player's two cards must consist of an Ace and a face card (King, Queen, Jack, or 10).

But importantly, before getting paid 1.5 times their wager, the player must also beat the dealer. If the dealer also has a blackjack, then the player and the dealer tie and the player doesn't win or lose any money on that hand.

As you might expect, players don't like to receive zero payout when they have the best hand in the game. Casinos understand this, and as a result, they have added a little wrinkle to the game that capitalizes on this fact and tilts the advantage slightly further in their favor. This wrinkle is known as "Insurance."

If the dealer's face-up card is an Ace, every player has an option to place a side bet known as "insurance." The insurance costs 50% of the players total bet. If the dealer ends up having a blackjack, the player gets paid out on the side insurance bet. Most of the time, players ignore the insurance option, but when a player has a blackjack of their own, risk aversion rears its ugly head and leads to poor decisions.

Imagine for a moment the following scenario: A player places a $100 bet. The cards are dealt, the player gets a blackjack, and the dealer has an Ace face up.

Since the player has blackjack, he or she stands to win 1.5 times the amount of their wager ($150). However, if the dealer has blackjack, the player will tie the dealer and win nothing.

Since the dealer has a face up Ace, the dealer will give the player the option to purchase insurance. The insurance bet would be for one half of the original wager ($50). In casino parlance, taking insurance under these circumstances is known as "even money" because the net effect of buying insurance is that the player will win an amount exactly equal to his original bet.*

A guaranteed payout on your original bet, sounds like a pretty good deal, right?

Wrong.

Yet, many players consistently take the insurance and the "even money" in this situation, and the reason is risk aversion.

Risk aversion deals specifically with decisions made under uncertainty. In those uncertain situations, such as a blackjack game, risk averse people tend to accept less risky alternatives with lower expected returns.

Players who take the insurance are choosing a lower, but more certain expected return ($100) over a higher, but less certain, expected return ($103.84). For a player who consistently makes $100 wagers, every time they take the "even money" their risk averse decision effectively costs them $3.84 tilting the odds toward the casino and away from the player. †

---

* For a $100 bet: If the dealer has blackjack, the player would push on their original hand ($0), and win on their insurance side bet (+$100) resulting in a net gain of $100. If the dealer does not have blackjack, the player would be paid at 1.5 times on their original bet (+$150), but they would lose their insurance side bet (- $50) for a net gain of $100. The "even money" insurance bet essentially guarantees a $100 win for the player.

† For those interested in the Expected Value calculation, please see the table in the footnote on the following page.

While taking the insurance and the "even money" illustrates risk aversion, three other aspects of the example illuminate the degree to which risk aversion can influence decision making.

First of all, and rather ironically, risk aversion manifests even in people who have willingly made the risky decision to gamble in a casino on blackjack. One could argue that these people are likely more risk loving by nature having decided to gamble as a source of enjoyment. Yet, even among risk-loving gamblers, risk aversion often finds a way to adversely influence decision making.

Second, even people who plan to gamble for many days or even weeks will take the insurance. In a one-shot deal, a player would end up with $100 from taking the even money and either $0 or $150 if playing out the hand. However, if that player plays for a long while, they will encounter the

Option:	Take the Insurance "Even Money"	Refuse the Insurance "Play out the hand"	
Dealer Hand:	Any dealer hand	If the dealer has Blackjack	If the dealer does not have blackjack
Payout:	$100	$0	$150
Odds of payout	1/1 (100%)	4/13[A] (30.8%)	9/13[B] (69.2%)
Expected return	$100 ($100 x 1)	$103.84 ($0 x 4/13) + ($150 x 9/13)	

A: There are 13 cards in the game, and only 4 of those will give the dealer blackjack (10, J, Q, K).
B: Of the 13 possible card values, 9 will not give the dealer blackjack (A, 2, 3, 4, 5, 6, 7, 8, 9).

same decision numerous times and their actual return will converge to the expected return.

If one plays blackjack long enough, they will undoubtedly do better by turning down the insurance. Yet, even for binge gamblers who plan to play a week's worth of blackjack, risk aversion often overcomes rational decision making.

Lastly, and perhaps most compelling, people will often take the insurance bet even when they know and acknowledge that it is a "sucker's bet." In casino parlance, bets with poor odds for the player are often referred to as "sucker's bets." With the insurance side bet, the casino agrees to pay 2:1 odds in the event of a dealer blackjack. Since 9 of the 13 possible cards result in the dealer not having blackjack, the casino has essentially agreed to pay the player 8:4 (or 2:1) on a 9:4 event. Seasoned players know these odds and appropriately refer to insurance as a "sucker's bet." Yet, these same players, driven by risk aversion, will often take the even money.

Risk aversion is so deeply ingrained that even risk-loving gamblers who clearly understand that the odds are stacked against them, consciously make poor long run decisions. If risk aversion can influence a risk-loving gambler, imagine the influence it can have on everyday decisions.

Outside the casino, risk aversion exerts a near all-encompassing influence on virtually every decision people make. People must decide what things to purchase, how to invest their savings, which career path to pursue, how to raise their children, and how to spend their leisure time. If risk aversion can sway the decision of a gambler engaging in a risky venture for fun, imagine the impact it can have on an average individual's decision about their investment portfolio or career choice.

Most of the time, people make these everyday decisions completely unaware that risk aversion influences their thinking. Unlike in a casino, the odds and payouts aren't clearly defined, and yet, people must choose between a wide array of options in all facets of their life.

In every one of these decisions, a person faces a tradeoff between two or more courses of action. When making the decision, risk aversion tends to influence people toward the lower risk, lower return option.

Like the instinctual forces that compel sardines to join in the shoal, risk aversion draws people in and binds them to the group. People avoid venturing out and away from the safety of the collective and exposing themselves to risk. This confines people to the metaphorical shoal and prevents them from making the bold decision to break free from the collective and zag.

CHAPTER 15

THE PARADOX OF INACTION

"Often the difference between a successful person and a failure is not one has better abilities or ideas, but the courage that one has to bet on one's ideas, to take a calculated risk - and to act."

— Andre Malraux

People avoid taking risks to prevent experiencing loss. People mistakenly reason that inaction will protect them. But instead, their inaction, while guarding from loss in the short term, often leads to long term disaster. This is the Paradox of Inaction.

In business, executives fall into this paradoxical trap all the time. Successful businesses with large market shares often opt for the perceived lower risk paths of passivity and deference. These market leaders possess the technological expertise, financial resources, and market access necessary to create the next big innovation. But successful innovation often comes with a cost. Those new products have the potential to make the old, profitable ones obsolete.

We saw this phenomenon with the new mail-order DVD Netflix model that destroyed the old video store

Blockbuster model. In this case, Blockbuster fell victim to the Paradox of Inaction. They could have acted and purchased a fledgling Netflix company. They could have acted and created their own mail-order business. But they didn't.

Creating a new model would have led to destruction of their successful old one. Action would have reduced their short-term profits. Blockbuster deftly avoided the short-term risk, but they failed in the long-term through inaction.

The Paradox of Inaction persistently threatens all successful companies and industries. And this failure to take calculated risks and act has ruined many successful companies including an iconic American business, Eastman Kodak.

Inventor and marketer George Eastman founded Eastman Kodak in 1889 in Rochester New York. The company grew quickly behind strong innovation and marketing efforts that delivered squarely against emerging consumer needs. Early inventions including the film roll and the Kodak camera, first launched in 1888, created the entirely new market of amateur photography.

For the next few decades, Eastman Kodak would continue to innovate and advance its current product line by improving performance, size, and capabilities of its cameras and film. The company also proved a savvy marketer, developing effective slogans such as "You press the button, we do the rest." Kodak expertly cultivated a highly profitable business model where the company sold cameras for low prices to drive broad penetration and made fat margins on sales of the photographic film.

Their innovation and marketing strategies proved wildly successful. In 1930, Eastman Kodak stock was added to the Dow Jones Industrial Average (DJIA), a powerful symbol of Kodak's preeminent status among United States companies. By 1976, Kodak held a seemingly insurmountable lead with a 90% market share of film sales and 85% share of camera sales in the large and lucrative US market.

But the great Kodak empire wouldn't last forever. Starting in the late 1990s, Eastman Kodak's once venerable stock began a long, slow, painful descent into oblivion. By 2004, Kodak's stock was removed from the DJIA. Less than a decade later, on January 19, 2012, Kodak filed for Chapter 11 Bankruptcy protection. The stock of an iconic company was now essentially worthless.

Kodak died a slow and painful death because it failed to act and enter the digital photography market. In late 1999, in an interview with the *New York Times*, former Kodak CEO George M. C. Fisher shed light on the issue: "And it [Kodak] regarded digital photography as the enemy, an evil juggernaut that would kill the chemical-based film and paper business that had fueled Kodak's sales and profits for decades."

Kodak viewed digital photography as the enemy that would destroy their highly profitable legacy camera and film business. As a result, they avoided the risk associated with entering the digital market, and suffered the long-term cost of protracted market share declines and obsolescence.*

---

* Kodak made other missteps along the way. Seldom is the downfall of large empire attributable to just a single failure. Kodak suffered

Kodak wasn't the first company, nor will they be the last, that suffered a similar fate. But Kodak's demise is particularly interesting for a few extraordinary reasons.

First, Kodak had a legacy of taking successful bold actions. Twice before in its history, Kodak had acted decisively and killed an old cash cow in favor of a new technology. Initially, Eastman's company focused exclusively on the commercial manufacturing of "dry plates" for professional photographers. Eastman's invention and marketing of "film roll" was the disruptive technology that made the former cash cow "dry plate" obsolete. Later, Eastman would invest in color film. At the time, color film didn't deliver the quality of black and white, but Eastman boldly invested in a new technology that would essentially wipe out the black and white market where Kodak, at the time, drew the lion's share of its revenue.

Second, Kodak didn't fail because they lacked the technological expertise. In fact, in 1975, Kodak engineer Steve Sasson invented the very first digital camera.

Third, Kodak didn't fail because they lacked time or understanding of the future marketplace. In 1981, following rival Sony's launch of the first commercial electronic camera, Kodak completed a market assessment on the future of digital photography. They concluded that digital could displace film in 10 years.

---

from a costly and failed pharmaceuticals venture and from a bloated cost structure. Nonetheless, the core reason for the downfall of one of the world's most successful companies was risk avoidance.

In the 1980s and 1990s, executives at Kodak didn't act with the vision or boldness of the company's founder. They possessed every advantage. They had the technology, an accurate market forecast, time to take action, a venerable brand, deep pockets, and they operated in a company that made the same leap twice before.

It was not technological acumen or an incorrect projection for the future that led to Kodak's demise – it was fear. They chose risk avoidance. They chose inaction.

Kodak executives could have acted boldly and replaced their dying, yet profitable film business. Unfortunately for Kodak's shareholders, the old cash cow of film proved too rich for Kodak executives to slaughter.

When Steve Sasson shared his invention with Kodak's upper management, they told him "That's cute – but don't tell anyone about it." Instead of taking a calculated risk, Kodak executives chose short term safety. Paradoxically, to avoid risking their old profit engine, they let their entire company die.

But Kodak doesn't stand alone. Encumbered by fear, every year, countless executives unwittingly sentence their companies to a slow and painful death from protracted sales and market share losses. Paradoxically, their intent to avoid lost sales ultimately leads them down this fateful path. And in the long-term, the company ends up worse off than if they had fully embraced the "riskier" alternative in the first place. This is Paradox of Inaction.

CHAPTER 16

GREEN REVOLUTION

"Dr. Borlaug has saved more lives than any other person who has ever lived."

– *Public Law 109-395* enacted by the US Congress to award a congressional gold medal to Dr. Norman E. Borlaug in 2006

Not many know the name Dr. Norman Ernest Borlaug. Yet, Dr. Borlaug may have saved more lives than any other person in world history. His work has saved over 1 billion from starvation. And his scientific advances have saved more land from deforestation than any environmental initiative. For his efforts, he is one of only seven people to have earned the Nobel Peace Prize, the Presidential Medal of Freedom, and the Congressional Gold Medal.*

---

* The others include: Martin Luther King, Jr. (American civil rights leader), Elie Wiesel (Holocaust survivor and novelist), Mother Teresa (Roman Catholic nun and missionary), Nelson Mandela (Anti-apartheid political prisoner and first democratically elected President of South Africa), Aung San Suu Kyi (Burmese democracy champion

Born in tiny Cresco, Iowa and raised on his family's farm, Dr. Borlaug would eventually achieve incomparable success. Dr. Borlaug was highly intelligent and an extremely hard worker. But it was his willingness to take a calculated risk that enabled him to stand apart and achieve greatness.

Borlaug didn't shy from risk or challenge in his life. As a youth, he could have stayed at home and worked on the family farm as most small town farm boys did in the 1930s. Instead, he ventured out of the small town and pursued a college education.

At the University of Minnesota, he competed on the varsity wrestling team, facing formidable adversaries in physical contests never shying away from a challenge. For his accomplishments on the mat and for his efforts to spread the sport throughout Minnesota, Borlaug would earn induction into the National Wrestling Hall of Fame.

After fighting his way through college, frequently putting his classes on hold so that he could earn money to survive, he took a job at DuPont as a microbiologist.

Following the Japanese attack on Pearl Harbor, Borlaug tried to enlist in the military. Again, he was not one to shy away from a challenge or afraid to take a risk. But the US government rejected his application. They had other plans for Borlaug including converting his lab into a research facility to help in the war effort. During this time, Borlaug and his team made important contributions to the Allied victory.

---

and political prisoner), and Muhammad Yunus (Bangladeshi social entrepreneur).

In 1944, after finishing his war service at DuPont, he made a decision that would forever alter the course of history. He turned down a stable and lucrative career with DuPont to pursue a startup wheat research and production program in Mexico.

He was young. He had a young child and a pregnant wife. In one hand, he held an offer from a great company in DuPont who promised to double his salary. On the other hand, he had an opportunity to pursue an undefined, but potentially amazing opportunity in Mexico with unlimited upside potential.

If put into Borlaug's shoes, most people, including the Kodak executives, would chose the low risk alternative with the certain short term payout. Fortunately for the billions of people whose lives he saved, Borlaug took a longer-term perspective and took a calculated risk.

Borlaug's fearless and visionary decision to take a calculated risk led him to Mexico. There he would face other difficult choices. And he would need to take more calculated risks to achieve success.

In Mexico, Borlaug's research focused on increasing wheat production. To achieve their goals, Borlaug and colleagues experimented with thousands of crossings of wheat varieties attempting to increase yields and improve resistance to crop diseases.

Progress was slow at first, but then Borlaug had a revolutionary idea. He theorized that he might be able to take advantage of the diversity of growing seasons within Mexico. Because of Mexico's geography and climatology, Borlaug posited that two growing seasons could prove suitable for growing wheat. His idea involved growing wheat in the central highlands in the summer, and then, immediately following that growing season, taking the seeds north and planting them near his research station in the Yaqui Valley. If it worked, he would dramatically increase output.

It was a great idea, but it flew directly in the face of established scientific beliefs.

First, Borlaug's idea challenged conventional thinking on photoperiodism. Scientists believed that specific wheat varieties couldn't effectively adapt to new environments, specifically seasonal changes in day length. Because of this issue, the idea would prove costly requiring extensive breeding efforts. Second, most agronomists believed that seeds needed a rest period to store energy before being planted.

According to widely held scientific beliefs, Borlaug's idea would surely fail. As a result, his boss vetoed the plan.

Borlaug faced another inflection point in his career. As an expert in the field and based on his experience and insights, he believed that his new approach could work. He could have backed down, but he didn't.

He took another calculated risk.

He resigned.

In was a risky gambit, but a well-considered one. He believed strongly in his approach. And he knew that his boss couldn't easily replace his contributions to the project. Borlaug's calculated risk worked. His boss acquiesced and gave him permission to proceed with his idea.

Borlaug tried the new approach. And it worked wonderfully crushing the long held conventional wisdom. Borlaug created the double wheat season.

But Borlaug didn't stop. In addition to the double-season approach, Borlaug developed shorter semi-dwarf varieties with thicker stems that could hold more wheat seed without crumbling under their own weight. He also developed new strains and pioneered new agricultural techniques to increase disease resistance.

Borlaug arrived in Mexico in 1944, and by 1963, less than two decades later, 95% of all Mexican wheat crops grew from Borlaug developed varieties. The Mexican wheat harvest in 1963 exceeded the yield in 1944 by a factor of 6 to 1.

In the early 1960s, Borlaug started to spread his new techniques around the world. He took his methods and varieties to the Indian sub-continent and later to Asia. Over the subsequent decades, he took his ideas to developing areas in Latin America, Africa, and the Middle East.

Everywhere he went, yields grew larger than ever before.

Bellies were filled. Lives were saved.

In addition to saving lives, the improvements in crop yields saved immeasurable amounts of wilderness from conversion to farm land. In India alone, increased yields saved an area the size of California (~100 million acres). Worldwide, without high-yield techniques, society would have had to convert an additional two billion acres to farmland to feed the world's population. That equates to an area roughly the size of the United States saved because Borlaug took calculated risks.

This amazing explosion in agricultural productivity which saved so many lives from starvation and saved so much wildernesses is now known as the Green Revolution. Dr. Norman Borlaug was its Father.

CHAPTER 17

AMBUSH

"I wasn't worried, I was just terrified."

– Thomas Morstead, New Orleans Saints Kicker

On August 23, 2005, Tropical Storm Katrina formed over the Bahamas, and at the time, most didn't anticipate the monstrous devastation she would inflict. Over the next seven days, the storm would grow into Hurricane Katrina, traverse the state of Florida, strengthen substantially while crossing the Gulf of Mexico, and then slam into the American Gulf Coast. Ultimately, Katrina would claim 1,836 lives and prove the costliest hurricane in United States history with damages estimated at over $80 billion.

Katrina ravaged New Orleans as the city's levee system failed resulting in catastrophic flooding. Over 90% of the area's inhabitants successfully evacuated, but 35,000 of those unwilling or unable to leave sought refuge in the New Orleans Superdome.

Opened in 1975, the Superdome is the largest fixed dome structure in the United States and serves as the home to the National Football League's New Orleans Saints. When Katrina crashed into New Orleans, the Superdome dutifully provided refugees protection from the raging winds and surging flood waters.

The 30-year-old structure took a violent beating from Katrina's category 5 winds. The terrible cyclone tore off chunks of the Superdome's roof and inflicted structural damage throughout the stadium. Despite the thrashing, the Superdome prevailed. She held strong and successfully defended the refugees from the devastating forces of Mother Nature.

Because of the massive damages, the Superdome had to close and undergo over $185 million of repairs. It would take a little over a year before the Superdome would host another football game. Then, on September 25, 2006, the stadium reopened when the home team New Orleans Saints hosted the Atlanta Falcons on Monday Night Football.*

The stadium, and more importantly, the Saints became a symbol of the city's undying spirit and resilience in the face of catastrophe. Just as the Superdome sheltered citizens giving them hope for survival, the Saints football team gave the city a welcome distraction from the ubiquitous misery and continuous struggle of rebuilding. The ailing city rallied around their beloved Saints who became a symbol of New Orleans' enduring spirit and a beacon of hope for the sons and daughters of New Orleans.

The Saints defeated the Falcons on Monday Night Football bolstered by unprecedented levels of fan support

---

* Monday Night Football is one of the marquee games of the week in the National Football League.

and behind new coach Sean Payton and new quarterback Drew Brees. The Saints would win their division that season and make the deepest push into the playoffs in franchise history before losing in the NFC Conference Championship game to the Chicago Bears.

A few years later, in the 2009 season, still carrying the hopes and dreams of a ravaged city, the Saints would post the best regular season record in franchise history and win Super Bowl XLIV earning the title of World Champion.* In doing so, the 2009 Saints again brought hope to a devastated, but recovering city and captured a world title for one the worst franchises in league history.†

However, the miracle season that culminated in a Saints' Super Bowl victory might have fallen tantalizingly short had Coach Sean Payton chosen the low risk alternative, played it safe, and acted conventionally. Fortunately, for the Saints and the city of New Orleans, Coach Payton zagged.

Super Bowl XLIV

Played in Miami, Florida, Super Bowl XLIV was the most watched event in United States television history with an average US audience of 106.5 million.‡ Television

---

* The 44th Super Bowl. The Super Bowl is the annual game between the champions of the two major conferences to determine the World Champion.
† Since coming into the league in 1967, the Saints had never even made it to a Super Bowl, and they only made the playoffs in 6 of the previous 42 seasons.
‡ The game eclipsed the record previously held by the series finale of M*A*S*H.

stations broadcast the game to nearly 40 countries around the world. The significance of the game and the far-reaching broadcast amplified the stakes, a dynamic that often increases risk aversion.

The game matched the underdog Saints with the favored Indianapolis Colts, owners of a league best 14-2 record led by arguably the best quarterback in the game, 10-time All-Star, Peyton Manning. After an evenly contested first half, the score stood at Saints 6 – Indianapolis 10.

To start the second half, the Saints had to kick the ball off to the Colts and their high-powered, Manning-led offense. If Manning could lead the Colts to a score on the first drive of the second half, they would take a commanding 17 – 6 lead. Coach Sean Payton had a decision to make.

Under the brightest of lights, with the whole world watching, Coach Payton pulled his team together and called a play that no other coach in Super Bowl history had called before. Coach Payton told his team: "We're running Ambush."

The Saints had practiced the play in the week leading up to the game, but the call was so bold and audacious that most players didn't think they would actually use it. Kicker Thomas Morstead, who would execute the critical first part of the play, would later tell reporters that upon hearing the decision from Coach Payton: "I wasn't worried, I was just terrified."

The play was a "surprise" onside kick to start the second half. For those not well versed in American football, an onside kick involves a very different approach than usual on a kickoff. During a kickoff, the kicking team (the Saints in this case) typically tries to kick the ball a long distance so that the returning team (the Colts) has a long distance to go to score a touchdown.

In an onside kick, the team kicks the ball a short distance and attempts to recover the ball themselves. After the kicked ball travels 10 yards, the kicking team can touch it, and if they recover it, they take possession of the football.

The play involves a great deal of risk for the kicking team. If they fail to recover, the receiving team will get possession with a relatively short distance to go to score a touchdown. However, if they recover, they'll have the ball in good scoring position themselves.

Coach Sean Payton knew the tradeoff that he faced. If the onside kick failed, Manning and the Colts would only have a short distance to go to extend their lead. If the attempt succeeded, the Saints would seize momentum and only have a short distance to score and take the lead. If the onside kick failed and the Saints lost the game, the criticism would be fierce and would linger for his entire career. His reputation was on the line. The hopes and dreams of New Orleans were on the line.

In the previous 43 Super Bowls, no one had attempted an onside kick before the 4th and final quarter. Onside kicks are typically reserved for the final quarter of the game, when the kicking team trails by a significant margin. In this context, the onside kick is deemed an acceptable desperation move to enable a late game comeback. But surprise onside kicks earlier in the game fly directly in the face of conventional wisdom. There is just too much at risk:

sacrificing field position, subjecting oneself to scathing criticism from the media and fans, and for some coaches, even putting their job in jeopardy. Coach Payton understood the tradeoffs and chose to eschew conventional thinking and zag.

At the start of the second half, the Saints successfully executed "Ambush." After recovering the ball at their own 42-yard line, the Saints marched quickly down the field and scored to take their first lead of the game. Buoyed by the momentum swing, the Saints won the game 31 – 17, capturing glory for themselves and the faithful fans of New Orleans.

Immediately following the bold decision, the crowd in attendance and the viewing public stood in amazement at the audacious call by Coach Payton. Veteran television announcer Jim Nance loudly proclaimed, "What a fearless start to the 2nd half."

Fearless indeed. But was it foolish?

Around the country, debates ensued. Was the call a careless gamble or a brilliant strategic decision?

A deeper examination of the actual odds of success seems to indicate that Coach Payton made a brilliant strategic decision. In fact, despite conventional wisdom that would indicate the contrary, the odds actually tilted in Coach Payton's favor. From 2001 to 2010, surprise onside kicks proved successful over 60% of the time!

Two factors contribute to the vast gulf between the conventional thinking and the reality of the situation. First of all, the success rate between "surprise" and "expected" onside kicks executed near the end of the game in desperation differs dramatically. While "surprise" kicks yield favorable results more than half the time, the much more common "expected" onside kick proves successful less than 20% of the time. On average, onside kicks are a losing proposition, but not when they are executed on an unsuspecting opponent.

Secondly, the conventional wisdom held among the coaching fraternity holds that failure's punishment is usually much worse than success's gain. In other words, the downside risk of ridicule and job insecurity outweighs the upside of winning a single game. This thinking, jaded by risk aversion, binds most coaches to the metaphorical shoal preventing them from executing a winning strategy. Thankfully for the Saints, Coach Payton was not tied to the conventional approach.

Importantly, Coach Payton had the Saints practice the "Ambush" play for the entire week leading up to the Super Bowl. Ambush wasn't a haphazard, last-minute decision to gamble. On the contrary, it was a well-considered, well-rehearsed execution of an under-utilized strategy.

Coach Payton made a difficult, but well-informed choice to go against conventional thinking, not just to be different, but in order to succeed. Coach Payton fearlessly did what so many coaches who came before him failed to do. He avoided falling victim to risk aversion amplified by the dramatic situation and worldwide stage, and executed the "surprise" onside kick.

Coach Payton zagged. The Saints won the Super Bowl. New Orleans, at long last, could rejoice.

CHAPTER 18

GO FOR IT!

"Man, cannot discover new oceans unless he has the courage to lose sight of the shore."

– Andre Gide

The kickoff isn't the only time when coaches underutilize a successful strategy. Coaches encounter another situation multiple times in every game. And, most of the time, when confronted with it, they take the lower risk alternative to the detriment of their team's chances of winning.

Imagine for a moment that you are the coach of an NFL team. Your team receives the opening kickoff and quickly drives the ball down the field. Eventually, you have the ball 4th and goal on your opponent's two-yard line.*You have a

---

* A team has 4 "downs" (or plays) to advance the ball 10 yards or the other team takes possession. On the 4th and final down, the conventional approach in most situation entails kicking a Field Goal or Punting (kicking) the ball to the other team. The punt is designed to push the opposing team further away from scoring. Instead of punting on 4th down, a team can choose to run another play and to try and gain the remaining distance and retain possession. Attempting a play on 4th down is colloquially known as "Going for it."

decision to make. Do you kick the field goal and take the almost certain 3 points? Or, do you go for it, and try to score the touchdown?

Based on probabilities from actual NFL games, the chance of scoring the touchdown on one play from the 2-yard line is approximately 3 in 7. This implies an expected payoff (or score) from going for it of 3 points (7 pts x 3/7 = 3 points). This is the exact same expected payoff from kicking the easy field goal. Given 4th and goal at the 2, a coach not influenced in any way by risk, and focused solely on maximizing points from this single possession should be indifferent between going for it and kicking the field goal.

But there is another significant advantage from taking the more aggressive position and going for it. If the touchdown attempt fails, the opposing team will take possession deep in their own territory, likely at the 2-yard line, in a precarious position. On the other hand, if the coach opts for the sure thing and elects to kick the field goal, the other team will receive the ensuing kickoff and likely take possession in much better field position, typically around the 20-25-yard line.

Many other factors complicate the decision for the coach – the current score, the time remaining, weather conditions, player morale, momentum, relative team strengths, and injury situation. But when coaches are confronted with a 4th and goal from the 2-yard line, they almost always kick the field goal.

David Romer, an economist at the University of California, studied the actions of coaches in 700 NFL games. In his sample, each and every time coaches were confronted with 4th and goal at the 2 yard they kicked the field goal.

This example makes an important point about risk aversion, but Romer's work went much further. In his study, Romer employed a mathematical technique known as dynamic programming to analyze 700 NFL games and determine the optimal choice to make at every position on the field.

Romer started by calculating the value of having a first down at every point of the field. Next, he determined the expected point value of a field goal attempt and the value created for the other team by punting.* Using the expected point values derived from his dynamic programming model, Romer determined the optimal, "win-maximizing" choice for the coach in every game situation.

Romer compared the win-maximizing choices with the actual choices made by NFL coaches and found a vast and statistically significant chasm. He found that coaches consistently chose to punt or kick field goals when they should have gone for it. Coaches "played it safe" and elected risk-averse, conservative choices reducing their team's chance of winning. In total, he found 1,068 4th down situations in which win-maximizing teams should have

---

* Along the way, Romer made careful choices to improve the validity of his findings. For example, when calculating the value of a first down, Romer focused on the 1st quarter to reduce complications that might arise from end of half or end of game situations. Additionally, he used an extensive sample of data including every game from three full NFL regular seasons.

gone for it. In those situations, teams only went for it 10% of the time (109 times) and kicked it 90% (959 times).*

Many NFL executives and coaches scoff at Romer's findings. They stress the importance of factors such as momentum in determining the outcome of a football game. They criticize some of the more "extreme" situations where Romer's modeling suggests teams should go for it such as 4th and 3 at the team's own 10-yard line. They reason that a failed attempt would result in a dramatic momentum swing deflating their team while emboldening the opposition.

Clearly, coaches do need to consider factors beyond pure mathematics when making game day decisions. The desire to avoid negative and decisive momentum swings partially explains why coaches don't always make decisions in line with Romer's recommendations. Some coaches, especially ones with precarious job security, will opt for the lower risk alternative for fear of drawing the ire of fans or their bosses. But, even after considering these factors, coaches appear to systematically make staggeringly conservative decisions.

---

* At a high level, the recommendations for coaches who want to maximize their team's chances of winning are as follows. On a team's own side of the 50 yard line, one should go for it when there are less than 4 yards to go. At the opponent's side of the field, the decision is a bit more complicated as the value from punting falls and the odds of a successful field goal attempt increase the closer one gets to the opponent's end zone. At the opponent's 45 yard line, one should go for it when it is less than 6.5 yards to go. The distance where a team should go for it then increases until peaking at 9.8 yards at the opponents 33. As the field goal becomes a sure thing, the distance contracts to a minimum of about 4 yards at the 21-yard line. From that point forward, the distance continues to increase, until inside the opponent's 5-yard line, when it almost always makes sense to go for it.

In defense of the NFL coaches, they face a difficult challenge. Risk aversion is a powerful force, deeply ingrained in our psyche that exerts a nearly pervasive influence on people's lives and decision making. Like the gamblers who take insurance, the coaches might even know the best decision to make, yet fail to make it. In close situations, coaches may fear the loss of a failed conversion more than they value the gain of a successful attempt. These coaches, fearful for their jobs and not wanting to face criticism for taking an unconventional approach, succumb to risk aversion and take an overly conservative approach to the detriment of their teams.

For those able to overcome risk aversion, the rewards are great. In Super Bowl XLIV, Coach Payton didn't follow the conventional route propelling his team to victory. But Sean Payton isn't the only football coach in the United States who has shunned risk aversion to execute an underutilized strategy. On a much smaller stage, Coach Kevin Kelley of the Pulaski Academy High School from Little Rock, Arkansas makes Coach Payton appear risk averse by comparison.

Coach Kelley's Pulaski team hasn't attempted a punt since 2007 and his team executes an onside kick on nearly every kickoff. Both strategies fly directly in the face of conventional football thinking, but Coach Kelley believes the odds are in his favor. If success is the measuring stick, Coach Kelley's 152-22-1 record and 5 state titles validate his unconventional approach.

None of what Coach Kelley does is haphazard. He bases his decision to employ "unconventional" tactics on probability assessments. His decision to forego punting and go for it on every 4th down has a rational basis substantiated by Romer's work.

Regarding onside kicking every time, Kelley has done his own math. In his experience, on average, a regular kickoff results in the opponent having the ball at their own 33-yard line. If an onside kick fails, the opponent usually gets the ball at their own 48-yard line. Given that Pulaski typically recovers 25% of their onside kick attempts, Kelley reasons that he sacrifices just 15 yards of field position (48-33) to get a 1 in 4 (25%) chance of getting the ball back. *

Kelley's approach strongly favors maintaining possession of the football. He attempts to get another possession via an onside kick. He tries to extend possessions by going for it on 4th down. Both of these atypical decisions are highly consistent with Romer's modeling that demonstrates the superior value of maintaining possession over small changes in field position.

Coach Kelley was once asked why he doesn't play by "the book." He responded: "Which book are you talking about? The one everyone uses, or the one that is right?"

In this context, "the book" is the conventional wisdom, the approach typically followed by most people, most of the

---

* 25% success for expected onside kicks is higher than the rate typically experienced by NFL teams. There are two important considerations in understanding the difference. First, opposing high school teams aren't nearly at skilled at fielding the onside kicks as NFL teams. Second, and much more interestingly, is that Pulaski practices onside kicks extensively and has numerous onside kick plays in its playbook. By choosing to employ the underutilized strategy consistently, Coach Kelley has trained his team to do something better and with more consistency than other teams.

time. Coach Kelley questioned that conventional thinking, and he made a bold and calculated decision to follow a different path. Coach Kelley zagged.

CHAPTER 19

BURN THE BOATS

"Alea iacta est."
"The die is cast."

– Julius Caesar

In January 49 BC, Roman General Julius Caesar faced a critical decision. General Caesar recently completed the conquest of Gaul expanding the Roman Republic's reach to include most of modern day France and Belgium. While still in Gaul, Caesar's term as Governor expired. This prompted the Roman Senate to order Caesar to lay down his arms, disband his army, and return to Rome.

Those directions came from Pompey, Caesar's former friend and close military and political ally. Roughly a decade earlier, Pompey, Caesar, and Marcus Licinius Crassus joined together in an alliance known at the First Triumvirate, an unofficial military-political alliance which used its influence in the Roman Senate to further its member's military, political, social, and financial agendas.

Overtime, Caesar and Pompey's relationship fractured. The death of Crassus in 53 BC and Julia Caesaris, Caesar's daughter and 4th wife to Pompey in 54 BC created a chasm in the relationship. That gulf grew wider as Pompey, roughly 15 years Caesar's senior, spent his time in the Roman Forum torn between squabbling factions of Senators while Caesar actively grew his fame as a conquering military hero.

In 51 BC, Pompey decreed that Caesar could not hold the position of Roman Consul without surrendering control of his army. Later in 49 BC, the Senate ordered the conquering hero to return to Rome. It was a risky gambit for Pompey – one that created a critical and vexing decision for Caesar.

Caesar led his troops to the northernmost border of the Roman Republic. There, on the northern banks of the River Rubicon, Caesar contemplated his next move. On one hand, he could stay in Gaul and attempt to hold his army together. But this would make him a nomad, a man without a country. Caesar, the quintessential Roman, likely felt revulsion from the mere thought of a life in exile from Rome.

Alternatively, Caesar could disband his army and return home as ordered by the Senate. Without his men, Caesar, who had many enemies, would find himself defenseless. If one of his enemies didn't kill him, one of his old friends would shortly upon arrival in Rome.

This left one final option for Caesar to consider, the option he would eventually choose. Ultimately, it was the only real option a man like Caesar would accept.

Caesar chose to cross the River Rubicon with his army and march toward Rome. From the moment, he crossed, he effectively declared civil war. The war pitted Caesar and his men against Pompey's formidable forces. Control of the Roman Republic hung in the balance.

Caesar fully understood the ramifications of crossing the Rubicon. Upon making his choice, Caesar famously proclaimed, "Alea iacta est" or "The die is cast." His declaration evidences his appreciation for his predicament and the irrevocable decision he just made. Once a die is cast in a gambling game, the gambler cannot take back the throw of the die. The die will eventually land on a number, but from the moment the die is tossed, an irrevocable wager has been made – the bell cannot be unrung, the die cannot be uncast. Caesar's metaphorical die had only two outcomes: win or die.

Pompey had backed Caesar into a corner. In the final analysis, Caesar had only one viable option. In the vernacular of ancient Chinese military strategist Sun Tzu, Pompey had put Caesar on "death" or "desperate" ground. In his epic treatise on military strategy, *The Art of War*, Sun Tzu identified 9 distinct "grounds," or battle situations, and offered a recommendation to the aspiring military tactician on how to lead forces in each circumstance. When a general finds his forces on desperate ground, there is only one alternative to death. Accordingly, Sun Tzu's advice is succinct: When on desperate ground, Fight!

And fight Caesar did. But more importantly, he got his men to fight for their lives. Once his men crossed the Rubicon with him, they too faced the same two possible fates: win or die.

Caesar brilliantly did to his men what Pompey had unwittingly done to him. Caesar placed his men on desperate ground with only one alternative to death – to fight for their lives. For when they crossed the Rubicon, Caesar had led them across the point of no return. Beyond that point, they would have no choice but to fight for their lives for Caesar. Caesar and his men had made an irrevocable strategic commitment – a powerful decision that would propel them to victory.

Making an irrevocable strategic commitment to inspire military performance was not a novel approach, especially for a military strategist of Caesar's caliber. This type of strategy was employed as early as 207 BC at the Battle of Julu which pit the Chinese Qin Dynasty against the rebel forces of Chu.

Facing an army roughly four times the size of his own, commander Xiang Yu famously commanded his forces to "Break the kettles and sink the boats." Specifically, he ordered that his men only carry three days of food and supplies and to destroy the rest including sinking their boats, the only means of retreat. With no way to retreat and limited food, Yu's inferior force fought for their lives and won victory for the Kingdom of Chu. Decades later, Greek and Roman military leaders, possibly even Caesar himself, "burned bridges" or scuttled ships to compel their forces to fight fiercely for their lives.

Crossing the Rubicon accomplished for Caesar what breaking the kettles and sinking the boats did for Xiang Yu. Caesar's men marched with great haste toward Rome. In fact, they marched so fast that they nearly beat the messengers dispatched from the Rubicon to inform Pompey and the Senate of Caesar's decision. Despite possessing a much larger army, Pompey and many of his closest allies in the Senate fled Rome immediately. Caesar pursued and eventually caught and defeated Pompey. Meanwhile back in Rome, Caesar was named Dictator of the entire Roman Republic.

Pompey's strategic mistake of backing Caesar into desperate ground and Caesar's decisive move to make an irrevocable strategic commitment by crossing the Rubicon offer a valuable lesson. Leaders need to embolden their teams to act courageously in the face of fear. When confronted with a similar situation, an aspiring zagger can use a well-timed irrevocable commitment to achieve greatness.

CHAPTER 20

WE CHOOSE THE MOON

"We choose to go to the moon. We choose to go to the moon in this decade and do the other things, not because they are easy, but because they are hard."

– John F. Kennedy

John F. Kennedy, 35th President of the United States, made his own irrevocable strategic commitment in late May 1961. His bold actions would propel his country to the new frontier of science and help the United States succeed on what Kennedy called the "most hazardous and dangerous and greatest adventure on which man has ever embarked."

The prior month, April 1961, had been a particularly challenging one for Kennedy and the United States of America. On April 12th, The Soviet Union had just bested the United States by achieving another major milestone in the Space Race. The Soviets, having already beat the Americans by launching the first satellite into orbit with Sputnik in October 1957, successfully launched cosmonaut

Yuri Gagarin into orbit making him the first human in space.*

Just weeks later, Kennedy and the United States suffered a great embarrassment on the world stage as a result of the failed Bay of Pigs Invasion of Cuba. CIA funded counter-military forces invaded Cuba with Kennedy's authorization only to face defeat at the hands of Fidel Castro's army in just three days. The botched attempt to overthrow the leftist regime embarrassed Kennedy and damaged the United States' credibility.

This was a critical juncture in world history. The two great superpowers of the time, the United States and the Soviet Union, engaged in a protracted and ideological battle teeming with political, economic, and military tension.

The United States and its NATO allies championed Democracy. The Soviets and their Warsaw Pact comrades favored Communism. The world watched and evaluated the outcome of every military, economic, political, and technological confrontation between the two sides. Outcomes influenced the allegiances of people and countries. Both sides aggressively sought converts to their worldview to secure them as allies in the Cold War and in preparation for the terrifying prospect of third great global war.

At this critical juncture, Kennedy licked his wounds and contemplated his options.

---

* Just three weeks later, the United States would put Alan Shepard into space. However, he would not attain orbit, a feat that the United States would not achieve until John Glenn successfully orbited the Earth on February 20, 1962.

Progress in the Space Race evidenced a nation's scientific and technological advancement, transforming it into a referendum on ideological supremacy. Unfortunately for the US and Capitalism, the Soviets and Communism were winning the race.

Like Caesar, Kennedy had a decision to make. Caesar cast his die and crossed the Rubicon. On May 25, 1961, in a special address to a joint session of Congress, with the eyes of the world upon him, Kennedy committed to the moon:

> *I believe that this nation should commit itself to achieving the goal, before this decade is out, of landing a man on the Moon and returning him safely to the Earth. No single space project in this period will be more impressive to mankind, or more important in the long-range exploration of space; and none will be so difficult or expensive to accomplish.*

– JFK, A Special Address to Congress on the Importance of Space

It was an audacious goal.

Other than fighting in a World War, Kennedy's proposal required an unprecedented national commitment of incalculable effort and a risky devotion of time and resources to a singular cause. It presented an immense technological challenge and would require protracted effort regardless of certain setbacks from unforeseen obstacles.

Kennedy made this strategic and irrevocable commitment on the world stage. In his now famous speech,

Kennedy acknowledged, "We take an additional risk by making it [commitment to the moon] in full view of the world."

It was indeed riskier, but it was brilliant. In fact, it was essential for Kennedy to marshal the national commitment he required to achieve his daring goal.

On one hand, Kennedy could have kept the US on its current trajectory of small incremental improvement and slow progress: launch more satellites, adjust rockets, tweak guidance systems, and so forth. With a few breaks, the US might catch the Soviets. But most likely, the US would stay just behind them in the quest.

On the other hand, he could create a plan to surpass the Soviets. He reasoned that more of the same approach would likely fail to accomplish this goal, so he asked Vice President Lyndon B. Johnson to identify a path forward that would afford the US a chance to win.

Johnson recommended the moon, and Kennedy agreed. The combination of a decade long time horizon and an ambitious goal would give the US ample opportunity to surpass the Soviets. But the plan would only succeed if Kennedy could marshal unprecedented support, resources, and commitment for the project.

Kennedy's strategic commitment engendered the national resolve necessary to attain the moon. The steadfast determination proved strong enough to overcome major setbacks and catastrophic losses including a cabin fire that killed the entire three-man crew and the Command Module of Apollo 1. Despite the technological challenges and loss of life, the Apollo program soldiered on backed by the nation's ardent support.

In all, there were 17 Apollo missions, but Apollo 11 was the one that realized Kennedy's goal. On July 20, 1969, Apollo 11's lunar module touched down on the moon's surface. Roughly six hours later on the morning of July 21st, astronaut Neil Armstrong became the first man to walk on the moon's surface. A few days later on July 24th, Apollo's Command Module splashed down in the Pacific Ocean, safely returning all three US astronauts to Earth. The US had surpassed the Soviets and accomplished the once unimaginable goal of landing a man on the moon and returning him safely to Earth.

Kennedy overcame fear of great personal risk to make a bold, but calculated, decision to pursue the moon. However, for Kennedy to achieve his stated goal, he needed a nation to follow him. Like Caesar before him, he garnered the necessary support through the well-timed use of an irrevocable, highly viable, strategic commitment.

Kennedy zagged.

Post Script

Risk creates fear, and fear sentences many to a mundane existence in the shoal.

To zag, one must overcome the paralyzing force and move courageously away from the comfort of the shoal.

But there exists a critical distinction between acting courageously and zagging. Courage is necessary, but not sufficient to zag. Courage could include a gambler wagering one's life savings on a long shot in a horse race. Courage can include an inexperienced boxer challenging an experienced and superior opponent to a fight. In both cases, the gambler and the boxer exercise courage, but neither zags.

To zag, one must not only conquer fear, but do it with an expectation of success. Kennedy didn't arbitrarily choose the moon. He selected that challenge because the difficultly level and time horizon created sufficient opportunity to surpass the Soviets. Coach Payton didn't haphazardly execute the surprise onside kick. He studied the odds and then practiced in advance to ensure his team's brilliant execution.

To achieve greatness, these zaggers made unbiased assessments of risk and then courageously broke free from the conventional with expectation of success. After identifying the right opportunity, those who triumph over risk do exactly what Coach Kelley instructs his team to do on 4th down: They "Go for it!"

Part Four

Culture

CHAPTER 21

SECOND NATURE

"We shape our buildings and afterwards, our buildings shape us."

— Winston Churchill

For centuries, scientists have deliberated the relative importance of "nature" versus "nurture" in determining a person's physical and behavioral traits. "Nature" deals with innate qualities that people inherit from their parents, and "nurture" includes all the experiences a person has in his or her life. While scientists continue to debate which, factor is paramount, no one doubts that both nature and nurture exert a powerful influence.

When considering culture, one is dealing with the "nurture" side of the equation. From the moment, a person enters into a new group, organization, or institution, they begin a process of indoctrination into that collective.

Consider a newborn baby just entering the world. From the moment of birth, they are immediately washed over with a flood of culture. They see the environment they are born into – perhaps a hospital, a home, a hut. They see the interactions of the doctors, nurses, and family members. They hear a new language spoken for the first time as their mother holds them tightly and whispers lovingly into their ear. The deluge of cultural influences will saturate the baby's life from their birth onward. Over time, the influence of culture will become more deeply ingrained, strengthened everyday by countless influences, and continually reinforced by the behaviors and affirmations of those closest and most trusted such as family and friends.

From the baby's perspective, culture will not appear to have a delineated role as something separate and distinct from their heredity. It is all they have ever known, and to them it will appear timeless, intertwined inextricably with the rest of their being. It will feel innate. It will be second nature.

Culture impacts people's perceptions and expectations without them even realizing it. Take a look at the picture below and think about what you see.

Depending on where you were born and raised, you will perceive different things. Westerners will interpret the images as that of a family inside a house and the square above the woman's head as a window through which one can see a plant. In contrast, someone born and raised in East Africa may perceive a family sitting under a tree and will think the woman is balancing a box on her head. Neither interpretation is right or wrong – just different.

These cultural differences develop and become ingrained over the course of a lifetime. Completely subconsciously, culture shapes people's perceptions leading to very different interpretations of the exact same image.

Even in similarly economically advanced cultures, differences can be significant as demonstrated by the Michigan Fish Test. Researchers showed the image below to both American and Japanese participants and found stark differences in how perceptions and memory of the picture differed by culture.

Try for yourself. Take a look at the image for five seconds. Then look away and describe what you remember.

Americans remember and describe with great accuracy the largest three fish. But Japanese participants remember the surrounding environment with vivid detail and accuracy. When the researchers made slight changes to the image and presented it to the participants again, the Americans noticed changes to the size and location of the fish and the Japanese more readily noticed changes to the scenery. While both interpreted the scene similarly overall, the areas of focus shifted dramatically depending on culture. Neither is right or wrong. But they are different.

Culture is a powerful force, developed and pounded in deep over the course of a lifetime. It is so entrenched that is essentially innate – a second nature. Culture exerts a subconscious impact on the way people perceive and interpret the world, and therefore, continually influences the way people think and act. Because culture is shared by groups, people from the same culture tend to think and act the same way.

As with the sardines, the majority of conventional thinking driven by culture isn't entirely bad. Most of the time it is incredibly useful and necessary. Culture includes the shared languages that a given group utilizes for written and verbal communication. Without a shared language practice, effective communication would prove impossible. Similarly, other shared practices greatly increase the safety, efficiency, and quality of life for the group. Standard conventions such as agreeing to drive on the same side of the road, orienting maps in the same direction, and wiring light switches in the same manner in every building leads to far fewer car wrecks, efficient navigation, and well-lit rooms. Not bad.

Most of the time, thinking and acting as prescribed by cultural norms results in desirable outcomes. But not all the time. Often, people mindlessly and blindly follow cultural convention and fail to evaluate other options or consider the consequence of their rote behavior. Those unable to break free from their cultural trappings are destined to zig. While those able to recognize and then conquer cultural conventions bestow upon themselves the opportunity for greatness.

CHAPTER 22

SUPERIOR ORDERS

"Often it is not so much the kind of person a man is as the kind of situation in which he finds himself that determines how he will act."

– Stanley Milgram

In 1992, *A Few Good Men,* the Rob Reiner film starring Tom Cruise, Jack Nicholson, and Demi Moore achieved both box office and critical acclaim. In total, it grossed nearly $250 million at the box office and earned four academy award nominations including one for Best Picture. In the movie, Lieutenant Danny Kaffee leads the defense in the court martial of two Marines, Private First Class Louden Downey and Lance Corporal Harold Dawson, who stand trial accused of murdering a fellow Marine.

The court room drama owes its success to many factors, but perhaps chief among them is a series of exceptional dramatic and heated exchanges between Kaffee, the lead defense attorney played by Tom Cruise, and Colonel Nathan R. Jessep, Commanding Officer of the Guantanamo Bay Naval Base in Cuba played by Jack Nicholson. One of these exchanges includes the signature line of the movie when Jessep indignantly barks at Kaffee, "You can't handle the truth!"*

While not nearly as widely remembered as some of the dialog between Kaffee and Jessep, the following court room exchange between Kaffee and Lieutenant Kendrick, an officer acting under Jessep's command played by Kiefer Sutherland highlights the crux of the defense's case:

> <u>Kaffee (Tom Cruise)</u>: Yeah, but it wasn't a real order, was it? I mean it's peace time. He wasn't being asked to secure a hill or advance on a beach head. Surely a Marine of Dawson's intelligence can be trusted to determine, on his own, which are the really important orders and which orders might, say, be morally questionable? Lieutenant Kendrick? Can he? Can Dawson determine on his own which orders he's going to follow?
>
> <u>Lt. Kendrick (Kiefer Sutherland)</u>: No, he cannot.

Kaffee's defense strategy is simple, but the moral and social ramifications are complex. Kaffee argues that Dawson and Downey can't be guilty of murder because they were just following the orders of their commanding officer. When Lt. Kendrick ordered Dawson and Downey to give a fellow marine a "code-red" beating as an extrajudicial punishment for his poor performance, the two subordinates had no choice but to follow the orders of their commanding officer. After all, as Kendrick admits during

---

* Voted as the 29th greatest movie quote of all time by the American Film Institute.

his court room exchanges with Kaffee, Marines do not have the ability or authority to discriminate between orders from a commanding officer.

Later in the film, after being called to the stand to testify, Colonel Jessep chastises Kaffee who has never served in a battle zone: "We follow orders or people die. It's that simple." In the Marines, where people must have complete trust in the chain of command and frequently place their lives in jeopardy, orders must never be questioned, only followed completely and without delay. In this environment, in this culture, Dawson and Downey had no choice but to obey orders from their superior and execute the "code-red" beating.

In the end, Kaffee's defense strategy proves successful in defending Dawson and Downey against the most serious charge of murder. But Dawson and Downey are found guilty of a lesser charge and dishonorably discharged from service for conduct unbecoming a Marine.

It was an interesting defense strategy, but far from a novel one.

The Nuremberg Defense

Following the end of World War II, the victorious Allied Forces held a series of military tribunals in Nuremberg, Germany in which the military and political leaders of Nazi Germany where charged with War Crimes, Crimes Against Peace, and Crimes Against Humanity. The accused employed a defense similar to Dawson and Downey – a defense strategy that would become eponymous with the German city that hosted the tribunals. They argued that a subordinate should not be held responsible for actions that were ordered by a superior. Unlike Dawson and Downey, the defense strategy proved unsuccessful for the Nazis. The judges found most of the defendants guilty and sentenced them to death or life imprisonment.

After the war, a Nazi solider named Adolf Otto Eichmann managed to escape from US custody. He fled to Italy posing as a refugee before absconding to Argentina using a fraudulently obtained Red Cross humanitarian passport and fake Argentine Visa.

Eichmann remained at large until a daring capture by the Israeli intelligence agency Mossad. The Mossad tracked down Eichmann in Buenos Aires where he lived under the assumed name of Ricardo Klement. Agents carefully tracked Eichmann's routine and devised a plan to snatch him on his daily commute immediately after he got off his bus and before he began his walk home.

On the day, they planned to apprehend him, Eichmann arrived a half hour later than usual, placing the staked-out Mossad team in a precarious position. When he did finally get off the bus, the Mossad leapt into action. After wrestling Eichmann to the ground, they tossed him in a getaway car and narrowly escaped detection at a police check point where guards scrutinized their phony license plates.

After their narrow escape, the agents transported Eichmann to a secure location within Argentina. There they gave Eichmann a choice: instant death or trial in Israel. Eichmann chose the latter.

To deceive the Argentinean authorities and avoid a potentially protracted extradition process, the Mossad smuggled Eichmann out of Argentina by drugging him and disguising him as a flight attendant. Once successfully transported to Israel, the Israeli authorities indicted Eichmann on 15 criminal charges including Crimes Against Humanity and War Crimes.

During the trial, Eichmann employed the same defense as his predecessors did at Nuremberg. He argued that he abdicated his own conscious to follow the Führer, Adolf Hitler. Eichmann testified, "I never did anything, great or small, without obtaining in advance express instructions from Adolf Hitler or any of my superiors."

Eight months after the trail began, Eichmann received a fate similar to his peers did at Nuremburg. Death by hanging.*

Milgram Experiments

Born in 1933 in New York City to Jewish parents, Stanley Milgram quickly took a keen interest in Eichmann's trial. When the Eichmann trial started, Milgram was still four months shy of his 28th birthday and had only a year of wear on his newly minted Ph. D in Social Psychology from Harvard University. At the time, Milgram worked as a professor at Yale. There he would devise a study to answer some of the vexing questions raised by The Nuremburg Defense.

---

* To this date, Eichmann is the only civil execution ever carried out by Israel.

Milgram began his famous experiment just three months after the start of the Eichmann trial. Inspired by the troublesome nature of The Nuremburg Defense, Milgram set out to answer the following question: "Could it be that Eichmann and his million accomplices in the Holocaust were just following orders?" Perhaps they weren't bad, immoral people, but instead, they were essentially good and moral people who also fell victim to the Nazi authority.

To answer these questions, Milgram designed a test. In the test, a volunteer comes to the laboratory believing that they will be a participant in a learning study. When they arrive at the lab, they are given the role of "Teacher" and an actor pretending to be another volunteer is given the role of "Learner." A third person, the "Experimenter" is the authority figure who is in charge of the test.

The Teacher and the Learner are placed in separate rooms where they can hear but not see each other. The Learner is hooked up to an electric shock device, and the Teacher is given control over the device. This gave the Teacher the power to administer electric shocks to the Learner. The device didn't really deliver a shock, but the Teacher was tricked into believing that it did.

Lastly, the Experimenter takes his place in the room with the Teacher so that he can provide instructions. The test setup is depicted in the following diagram.

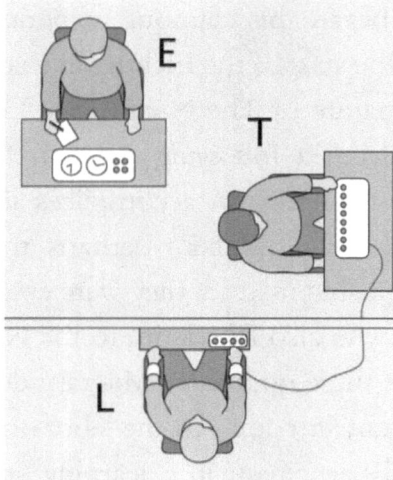

E = "Experimenter"; T = "Teacher"; L = "Learner"

Once the test participants were setup properly, the Teacher was given a list of word pairs to "teach" the Learner. The Teacher would read the first word of the pair, and the Learner would select a response from four possible answers. Every time the Learner provided an incorrect response, the Teacher would administer an electric shock to the Learner. These shocks increased in 15 volts increments with every additional incorrect answer.

To complete the ruse, a series of pre-recorded sounds including moans and screams of pain were played at each shock level. Additionally, the Learner, who was an actor, would sometimes bang on the wall, and in some versions of the test, he would complain about a heart condition.

If the Teacher asked the Experimenter to stop the test, the Experimenter would implore them to continue with a series of verbal prods. If the Teacher insisted on ending the test four straight times, the test was terminated. Otherwise, the test continued until the Teacher administered the maximum 450-volt shock three times.

In Milgram's initial test, 26 out of 40 (65%) of participants delivered the final 450-volt shock. While every one of them questioned the experiment at some point, the majority obeyed the Experimenter's verbal prodding and continued on with the experiment.

Amazingly, not a single person, not even those who refused to continue with the experiment themselves, left the room to check on the Learner without first requesting permission from the Experimenter. Moreover, none of the 14 objectors asked that the experiment itself be terminated. They just wanted the Experimenter to excuse them.

Milgram offered the following perspective:

> *Stark authority was pitted against the subjects' [participants'] strongest moral imperatives against hurting others, and, with the subjects' [participants'] ears ringing with the screams of the victims, authority won more often than not. The extreme willingness of adults to go to almost any lengths on the command of an authority constitutes the chief finding of the study and the fact most urgently demanding explanation.*
>
> *Ordinary people, simply doing their jobs, and without any particular hostility on their part, can become agents in a terrible destructive process. Moreover, even when the destructive effects of their work become patently clear, and they are asked to carry out actions incompatible with fundamental standards of morality, relatively few people have the resources needed to resist authority.*

In certain situations, few people can resist the orders of an authority figure even if they are in stark contrast to one's morals. Milgram's original experiment has been repeated many times, and with many variants. Remarkably, the percentage of people willing to inflict the highest voltage remains highly consistent.

While Milgram's findings don't excuse immoral behavior, they do provide a partial explanation for some wartime atrocities. This is particularly true in strong cultures where systematic indoctrination is designed to break down the individual and build up the group.

A similar dynamic exists in authoritarian and totalitarian cultures, where obedience to authority is demanded of individuals. In these situations, consistent with Milgram's research, people abdicate their own conscious to that of the group. When this happens, individual thought and morality often gets tossed aside in favor of blind obedience to the will of the collective.

Milgram's work and that of other researchers shows that obedience to authority appears to be a consistent phenomenon across time and across cultures. But when looking across cultures, there are significant differences in the way that this dynamic manifests. In military cultures, a well-defined chain of command prescribes the hierarchy. In authoritarian or totalitarian regimes, political, economic, and military power structures determine the social order and class structure.

In addition to determining who is superior and who is subordinate, culture also defines the nature of the relationship between members of society. Culture dictates the manner in which people interact, the level of deference given to authority figures, and the decorum and convention that guide societal interactions.

By determining the hierarchy of a society and the manner in which group members interact, culture obliges people to think and act similarly. As a consequence, people will tend to act in accordance with the norms that define their particular culture.

This bounded and conventional thinking can result in atrocious outcomes. In some cultures, in specific social settings, people can and will submit to the command of an authority figure, perpetrate horrible crimes, and inflict pain and punishment on fellow humans. They will do it blindly and without questioning, just like a sardine cleaves to a shoal, they follow regardless the outcome.

But as Milgram's experiments show, it doesn't take years of indoctrination for an average person to blindly follow an authority figure. Any day, anyone can become a sardine. *

---

* Have you ever heard of or played the game "Six degrees of Kevin Bacon?" For those who haven't, the challenge is to connect any actor or actress through their film roles to the actor Kevin Bacon in six moves or less. The parlor game is a variant of the "small world experiment" designed to calculate the length of social networks. That experiment was conducted by Stanley Milgram. And, in *A Few Good Men*, Kevin Bacon plays the role of the prosecutor Captain Jack Ross. In our small world, Milgram and Bacon are not only connected, they are intertwined.

CHAPTER 23

MANMADE DISASTERS

"People usually think according to their inclinations, speak according to their learning and ingrained opinions, but generally act according to custom."

— Francis Bacon

The Nazi war crimes demonstrate the horror that ordinary people can perpetrate against others when acting under the powerful influence of culture. But culture's expansive grip extends far beyond people from one group taking action against another. In fact, many times culture leads members of a group to continue down a path that will lead to their own demise or to the great detriment of the group they intend to protect.

In Japan, on March 11, 2011, a massive underwater seismic thrust known as the Tōhoku Earthquake initiated a series of events that would culminate in the second most devastating nuclear disaster in history. Mankind was helpless to prevent much of the damage resulting from the massive earthquake and ensuing tsunami. However, the resulting nuclear disaster could have easily been avoided had it not been for the Japanese culture.

It started roughly 43 miles off the East coast of Japan and approximately 20 miles deep in the Pacific Ocean. From these cold depths, the fourth most powerful earthquake in modern times rocked the entire planet.* The massive earthquake gave birth to an immense tsunami. Enormous waves, some measuring over 100 feet, slammed into the East coast of Japan. Some of those waves traveled over six miles inland leaving behind a trail of unimaginable destruction. Everything told, 15,893 would die and 2,572 go officially "missing." The World Bank estimated the total economic cost at $235 billion making it the costliest natural disaster in world history.

Japanese culture had no bearing on the actual earthquake and resulting Tsunami. The earthquake occurred as a result of the convergence of two of Earth's tectonic plates. For millennia, off the coast of Japan, the Pacific Plate has moved slowly, but steadily under an adjacent plate in a process known as subduction. In this process, the Pacific plate sinks into the Earth's mantle creating massive downward pressure on the upper plate. This stress builds up over time. Ultimately, that stress needs to be discharged. On March 11, 2011, the pressure released in a massive and unavoidable seismic event.

---

* Modern earthquake recording began in 1900. Measuring 9.0 on the Richter scale The Tōhoku Earthquake was the fourth largest in history. The force was so powerful that it actually shifted the axis of the Earth somewhere between 10—25 cm. The strongest earthquake ever occurred on May 22, 1960 in Valdivia, Chili measuring 9.5 on the Richter.

The Tsunami was inevitable. The Japanese were innocent victims who suffered devastating losses through no fault of their own. But the nuclear meltdown that followed at the Fukushima I Nuclear Power Plant could have been averted had it not been for the failings of the Japanese culture.

Like other accidents within complex systems, no single issue caused the meltdown. Rather, a chain of failures collectively resulted in the worst nuclear event since the 1986 meltdown at Chernobyl.

Sadly, according to an investigative committee appointed by the Japanese government: "the direct causes of the accident were all foreseeable prior to March 11, 2011." Even more painful, was the fact that after an exhaustive investigation the committee concluded that the Fukushima Daiichi nuclear disaster was a "profoundly manmade disaster." The committee elaborated:

For all the extensive detail, it provides, what this report cannot fully convey – especially to a global audience – is the mindset that supported the negligence behind this disaster.

What must be admitted – very painfully – is that this was a disaster "Made in Japan."

Its fundamental causes are to be found in the ingrained conventions of Japanese culture: our reflexive obedience; our reluctance to question authority; our devotion to 'sticking with the program'; our groupism; and our insularity.

Had other Japanese been in the shoes of those who bear responsibility for this accident, the result may well have been the same.

Not the earthquake. Not the tsunami. Not an individual. But instead, the investigative committee said that the Japanese culture was to blame.

To understand this unusual conclusion, one must understand a bit more about the history and regulatory structure of the Japanese nuclear industry. In the 1970s, in the aftermath of the global oil crisis, Japan accelerated its nuclear power program in the name of energy independence and national security.

Nuclear energy became a primary public policy goal which the Japanese pursued with dogged determinism. The nuclear industry had a powerful mandate unanimously bestowed by the government, the business sector, and the populist will to develop and flourish in the name of the greater Japanese good. The unwavering collectivist pursuit of a common goal is a defining characteristic of the Japanese culture. And following WWII, this collectivist determination drove Japan's economic miracle.

As the industry grew, a regulatory structure responsible for protecting the public interest developed in parallel. In its final report on the Fukushima disaster, the commission characterized the relationship between the regulators and the industry they were charged with regulating as *incestuous*. It was incestuous in critical ways that compromised the pursuit of public safety.

First, the governance hierarchy created a serious conflict of interest. Specifically, the Japanese regulatory agency (NISA) was created as part of Ministry of Economy, Trade, & Industry. The Ministry actively championed the virtues and safety of nuclear power. The regulatory agency NISA reported to the Ministry. In its final report, the committee chastised the absurdity of the governance structure of the Japanese Nuclear Industry: *"Its regulation was entrusted to the same government bureaucracy responsible for its promotion."*

Compounding the problem, the Japanese government staffed NISA with mostly non-technical bureaucrats. These appointed officials were typically not nuclear safety engineers. So, even if their interests weren't perverted, they still would have lacked the requisite technical skills to effectively govern the complex industry.

Second, a Japanese practice known as Amakudari exacerbated the snarling conflict of interest. In the common Japanese cultural convention, public sector bureaucrats commonly retire to high profile positions in the private sector. This created a complex and perverted incentive for NISA regulators. On one hand, they were charged with preserving public safety through regulation of nuclear power companies. On the other, they stood to benefit later in life from a high paying position at one of the companies they were charged with regulating.

In the end, for many, their ultimate allegiance rest with protecting the bureaucracy and the industry and not the safety of the public. Not only were these non-technical bureaucrats ill-equipped to regulate a complex industry, strictly enforcing regulatory standards could jeopardize their chances of securing a cushy executive job later in life.

The Japanese cultural phenomenon of Amakudari created incestuous blurring of the lines between the public regulatory bodies and private industry groups. This blurring, combined with Japan's strong collectivist determination to pursue nuclear power, formed a dangerous cultural cocktail that ultimately scarified public safety in the relentless pursuit of a perceived national imperative.

The Japanese regulators failed to enforce international safety standards adopted worldwide based on learning from previous nuclear incidents including Three Mile Island and Chernobyl. Despite knowledge of these issues and risks, the regulators permitted the facility to operate.

The NISA regulators and the TEPCO (Tokyo Electric Power Company) operators received several warnings about the safety of their facilities, but they chose to ignore them.

As early as 1991, the US Nuclear Regulatory Commission issued a warning about the plant's safety. The Japanese ignored the warnings.

In 2008, an internal TEPCO audit identified an immediate need to protect the plant from flooding from seawater in the event of a massive Tsunami. Top management reviewed the study, but they took no action. They claimed that such an event was extremely unlikely.

Also in 2008, The International Atomic Energy Agency issued strong warnings citing their concern that Japan's nuclear facilities would have serious problems withstanding earthquakes with magnitudes above 7.0. Again, TEPCO operators took no action, and NISA failed to effectively regulate.

In 2009, earthquake researchers implored NISA and TEPCO to reconsider their assumptions about the potential height of Tsunami waves. Operators and regulators did nothing.

The Fukushima facility was not reinforced or built strongly enough to withstand a massive earthquake. The plant was built far too close to the sea without adequate protections to prevent flooding in case of a Tsunami. If regulators would have required strict adherence to international standards, the facility would have been reinforced structurally or moved prior to the day of the Tōhoku earthquake. But they didn't. Amakudari blurred responsibilities and collectivist ambition obfuscated the risk.

Yet another Japanese cultural characteristic led to problems both before and after the Tsunami. Japan possesses a very hierarchical culture where "saving face" often supersedes clear and efficient communication.

Before the Tsunami, operators failed to report several small-scale accidents up the chain of command. Communicating accidents could lead to reprisal from a deeply respected superior. Communicating accidents also implied that future accidents, perhaps even more severe ones were possible.

Culture impeded the development of technology that could have proven extremely helpful in averting disaster. Despite possessing extraordinary technological acumen, the industry failed to develop robots that could diffuse critical situations preventing meltdown. They didn't pursue them for the fear that developing said robots would intimate that a meltdown situation was theoretically possible.

And, completely at odds with international standards, the plant operators had not been properly trained on how to react in a variety of situations. Perhaps training for natural disasters, such as flooding due to a Tsunami, appeared too close to an admission that flooding was possible. This lack of preparedness led to critical errors that compounded the problems in the days immediately following the Tsunami.

After the Tsunami, the hierarchical nature of the organization and tangled objectives of industry, government, and regulators crippled the speed of decision making. For even with a poorly reinforced facility built dangerously close to the sea manned by poorly trained operators, a full meltdown could have been averted if someone had made a quick decision to rapidly cool the reactors with sea water.

But making the decision took far too long. Hierarchy and face-saving paralyzed the decision makers. By the time the government ordered the cooling with sea water, full nuclear meltdown was inevitable.

CHAPTER 24

CULTURAL ADVANTAGE

"We hold these truths to be self-evident, that all men are created equal, that they are endowed by their Creator with certain Unalienable Rights, that among these are Life, Liberty, and the pursuit of Happiness. That to secure these rights, Governments are instituted among Men, deriving their just powers from the consent of the governed."

– The Declaration of Independence of the United States of America, July 4, 1776

Some individuals and groups don't fall victim to the trappings of culture. These people and companies, aware of existing cultural dynamics, make the purposeful decision to choose to change their culture or establish a new one.

For a software company named SAS Institute, it all started in 1976 when co-founder James Goodnight decided to give employees free M&Ms every Wednesday. What started as free M&Ms grew over the decades into one of the most expansive benefits packages offered anywhere in the world.

SAS employees now have access to countless on-site amenities including day care, preschool, a state of the art gym, a masseur, beauty services, social counseling, car detailing, and healthcare. SAS has doctors and nurses on-campus who provide routine healthcare for the entire family…for free.

The benefits don't end there. SAS employees receive cut rate memberships into Goodnight's country club, and they are encouraged to adhere to a 35-hour work week. There is no dress code. Fresh cut flowers, beautiful artwork, and harmonious music fill the campus. Not surprisingly, Goodnight's Cary, North Carolina based SAS Institute routinely ranks as one of the best companies to work for in America. And, in 2011, SAS was ranked the #1 place to work by Fortune Magazine on their prestigious listing of the "Best 100 Companies to Work For."

Today, many high technology firms have copied the SAS approach. In fact, Google, the reigning champion on Fortune's "Best Companies to Work For" and a long-time SAS customer modeled their expansive benefits program after Goodnight's. But SAS was one of the first to take the novel approach to employee benefits, and they have been doing it for over 30 years.

SAS is still a for-profit entity, and they profit handsomely. SAS has delivered consistent growth averaging a whopping 90% per year for over three decades. They have never experienced a loss. They have never been forced to lay off a single employee. And this consistent success has made founder James Goodnight one of the richest men in the world.*

SAS CEO Jim Goodnight's decision to build a unique culture has generated consistently impressive business results. Goodnight, like most other CEOs, aims to consistently increase his company's profits. He isn't just handing out jelly beans to employees for purposeless smiles.

In his particular industry, Goodnight realizes that his people are his largest asset. Goodnight reasons, "You know, I guess 95 percent of my assets drive out the front gate every evening. It's my job to bring them back."

And Goodnight does an exceptional job of bringing them back. Employee turnover at SAS averages about 3% compared to over 20% for the rest of the industry. This stark discrepancy confers numerous advantages to SAS. It provides SAS with significantly lower recruiting and training costs, and perhaps more importantly, it gives them a more seasoned employee base, a critical advantage when competing in a knowledge based industry.

The culture offers Goodnight more than low turnover. It also encourages creativity and innovation. SAS believes that happier, healthier employees with work-life balance develop better software with fewer mistakes. It stands to reason that a fresh and inspired software engineer could develop better code than one stressed out and run down from a long string of 80+ hour work weeks.

---

* In Forbes 2016 list of the richest people, Goodnight checked in at number 144 in the world and number 54 in the United States with an estimated net worth of $8.3 billion.

Extensive onsite amenities such as childcare, healthcare, fitness centers, and cafeterias serve a very practical purpose. By minimizing the sources of outside stress and distraction, SAS enables its employees to focus their efforts on the task of building complex software. Instead of having to juggle childcare, a software engineer can get exceptional and reliable service on site. The engineer doesn't need to worry about who will take care of the kids, only about writing exceptional code.

SAS employees don't need to drive to a doctor's appointment and then spend hours in waiting rooms to see the doctor. They can just stroll into the on-site facility and visit with a doctor immediately. This saves time and encourages more preventative care. SAS estimates the combined time savings and productivity gains at around $5 million per year.

Forty years ago, conventional wisdom held that employees are assets that should be squeezed for every drop of productivity. But Goodnight decided to take a different approach. He chose to establish a unique culture to keep his people happy, satisfied, and therefore more productive for the long term.

His purposeful decision enabled his firm to achieve outstanding success in a challenging industry. Currently, SAS has nearly $3 billion in annual sales and serves customers in 135 countries. In a knowledge based industry characterized by high employee turnover, Goodnight's novel approach conferred him a sustainable competitive advantage.

CHAPTER 25

CULTURAL ADVANTAGE v2.0

"Businesses often forget about the culture, and ultimately, they suffer for it because you can't deliver good service from unhappy employees."

– Tony Hsieh, CEO Zappos.com

SAS isn't the only company that developed a unique corporate culture to provide a competitive advantage. The story of Zappos.com provides another interesting perspective on the power of culture to deliver business results.

Founded in 1999 during the height of the ".com" boom, Zappos.com thrived when so many other fledgling companies failed. Today, Zappos.com sells billions of dollars of shoes, clothing, and apparel online. But Zappos.com could have easily become one of the thousands of companies who launched then quickly flamed out when the great internet bubble burst.

Yet, Zappos.com flourished. Why?

Co-CEO's Tony Hsieh and Nick Swinmurn decided to build the entire company around providing superior customer service. By offering exceptional service, they reasoned they could differentiate themselves from hordes of other online retailers who offered similar products at similar prices.

But building superior customer service is much easier said than done. This was especially true in internet sales. The customer service representatives for Zappos.com, like every other online merchant, would be call center employees. As anyone who has ever dialed into a call center knows, superior customer service is not a hallmark of the experience.

To differentiate itself, Zappos.com needed to build an army of highly engaged, knowledgeable, service-oriented representatives to provide outstanding customer service. It had to be done in an industry where good customer service was an exception, not the norm. Additionally, as a startup online merchant operating on thin margins, they couldn't afford to pay monstrous salaries to attract the talent they desired. They had to figure out a way to build a wonderful customer service machine sourcing from a labor force many would characterize as transient, distracted, and self-absorbed.

Zappos.com accomplished its goal by focusing on its culture. According to Tony Hsieh, "At Zappos, we really view culture as our No. 1 priority."

In an industry characterized by poor service delivered by disenfranchised employees, Hsieh reasoned that creating a great culture, one that stands apart from the rest, would drive results by "unleashing what people already have inside them that is maybe suppressed in most work environments."

Zappos.com starts the process of building its culture by selecting for it in the hiring process. Prospective employees must take two interviews. Similar to most companies, the first interview assesses the candidate's ability to do the job.

The second interview sets Zappos.com apart. In this discussion, the interviewer's focus is on assessing the candidate's personality and fit with the Zappos.com culture. Interviewers ask seemingly odd ball questions, but they all serve a specific purpose. The interviewers are trying to ferret out how well the prospective employee will adopt the Zappos.com core values.[*]

Once hired, new call center employees go through an extensive 4-week customer service training course where they learn to deliver the experience that Zappos.com expects. They practice service calls with real customers while being observed and coached by Zappos.com training staff. Finally, at the end of the 4-week training program, Zappos.com makes them an unusual offer.

Zappos.com offers its carefully selected and thoroughly trained new employees an offer to quit in exchange for cash. If they choose to quit, Zappos.com will pay them $2,000 – no questions asked. The remarkable offer serves an important purpose. It weeds out anyone not truly

---

[*] Zappos proudly claims the following 10 core values: 1) Deliver WOW Through Service (2) Embrace and Drive Change 3) Create Fun and A Little Weirdness (4) Be Adventurous, Creative, and Open-Minded 5) Pursue Growth and Learning 6) Build Open and Honest Relationships With Communication (7) Build a Positive Team and Family Spirit (8) Do More With Less (9) Be Passionate and Determined (10) Be Humble.

committed to embracing the company's core values and becoming part of the Zappos.com family.

Once part of the Zappos.com family, employees get the royal treatment. They get free health care, free lunches, and get to work in a fun and quirky environment. To ensure managers don't snuff out all the fun in the name of productivity, Zappos.com charges its managers with spending 10-20% of their time "goofing off" with their employees.

These happy and committed employees then go above and beyond the call of duty to provide exceptional customer service. Some of these customer service stories have become legendary. One employee spent 8 hours on a single customer call. Another sent flowers to the funeral of a customer's relative. These legends only fuel the fire of service-minded employees encouraging them to offer even more exceptional service.

Zappos.com prominently ascribes its success to a maniacal focus on service: "We've been asked by a lot of people how we've grown so quickly, and the answer is actually really simple... We've aligned the entire organization around one mission: to provide the best customer service possible. Internally, we call this our WOW philosophy."

Outstanding service differentiated Zappos.com from the hordes of other online merchants. This unusual and unexpected service quality has driven strong loyalty among current customers and generated word-of-mouth recommendations attracting new customers. Customer loyalty has driven tremendous sales growth which has created demand for more employees. And because of

Zappos.com's growing reputation as an outstanding employer, customer-service minded individuals flock to Zappos.com. This virtuous and self-perpetuating cycle has driven Zappos.com from start-up to a billion-dollar merchant in less than a decade.

Like SAS, Zappos developed a strategic competitive advantage by taking a different approach to building their corporate culture. Importantly, SAS and Zappos don't just hand out free M&Ms and lunches because it makes the leadership feel good. Leaders at both companies carefully assessed the nature of their specific industries, then took a series of mindful and intentional steps to create a sustainable advantage.

In a knowledge based software industry characterized by high turnover and burn out, Goodnight focused on improving employee satisfaction and reducing stress levels. As a result, SAS turnover is virtually non-existent and unencumbered employees churn out a robust flow of fresh and elegant code.

In the burgeoning online retail space typified by poor customer service and unpleasant call center experiences, Zappos.com developed a culture that enabled and encourages exceptional service to drive loyalty and sales growth.

Both companies used culture to their advantage. Their leaders were not bound by the typical business conventions that existed in their industries. They thought differently. They created unique cultures that conferred competitive advantage. They zagged.

CHAPTER 26

SPIRIT OF COMPETITION

"To bring about radical breakthroughs for the benefit of humanity, thereby inspiring the formation of new industries and the revitalization of markets that are currently stuck due to existing failures or a commonly held belief that a solution is not possible."

— Mission of the XPRIZE Foundation

In the decade following the Wright Brothers first flight, mankind made substantial aeronautical progress as entrepreneurs and sovereign nations alike pursued the heavens with competitive vigor.[*]

Less than 10 years after the first flight, and prior to WWI, several countries could build airplanes capable of delivering bombs to enemy targets. In 1911, Italy became the first country to use airplanes for a military purpose during the Italian-Turkish War (1911-1921). Bulgaria followed shortly thereafter during the First Balkan War (1912-1913).

---

[*] Orville and Wilber Wright made their famous first flight on December 17, 1903 just south of Kitty Hawk, North Carolina.

By WWI (1914-1918), airplane usage was widespread. Both Allied and Central powers made extensive use of airplanes to conduct reconnaissance, deploy bombs, and engage in aerial "dog fights." Mankind had made awe-inspiring progress in aeronautics in the short time since Orville and Wilbur made their famous first flight in 1903. This tremendous progress was propelled by a culture of competition.

After the first Great War, the competition continued. This time the spirit of competition was created by a New York hotel owner named Raymond Orteig. In a letter sent to the Aero Club of America, Orteig offered a cash prize of $25,000 to the first pilot from any Allied country to fly across the Atlantic Ocean between Paris and New York.

Nine teams of pilots attempted the transatlantic flight in an effort to claim the prize. Most teams incurred expenses many times greater than the cash reward. Collectively, the teams spent an estimated $400,000 in pursuit of victory. In three separate crashes, six men lost their lives. Eventually, in 1927, an unexpected champion, a US Airmail Pilot, emerged to conquer the Atlantic Ocean.

Charles Lindbergh made several unique decisions that contributed to his successful flight of the Spirit of St. Louis from New York to Paris. Lindbergh flew solo in a single engine plane unlike his competitors who opted for flight teams in tri-engine planes. He also bravely dispatched with all non-essential equipment to reduce weight.

Single engine reliance was risky. Flying solo for the entire 33.5-hour trip required extreme focus and endurance.

Proceeding without a radio, sextants, or parachute demanded both skill and courage.

On the day of his departure, Lindbergh encountered weather conditions that would have grounded many pilots. Lindbergh, sights set on capturing the Orteig Prize, took the risk and departed for Paris. Lindbergh would later remark: "I don't believe in taking foolish chances. But nothing can be accomplished by not taking a chance at all."

Lindbergh prevailed. But the real winner was the aviation industry.

Shortly after his return to the United States, Lindbergh went on tour. In less than three months, the national hero visited 48 states, delivered 147 speeches, and rode 1,290 miles in celebratory parades. Within one year, a full quarter of the US population, approximately 36 million people, laid eyes on Charles Lindbergh and the Spirit of St Louis.

Spurred by Lindbergh, the aviation industry began its great boom. In the US, the number of airline passengers increased 30 times from 1926 to 1929 (5,782 to 173,405). Before Lindbergh, the sky belonged to the gods, the birds, and the privileged few. After Lindbergh crossed the ocean named for Atlas, the Greek God who shoulders the Earth, the sky was no longer reserved for the gods. The sky was now the privilege of man.

The Orteig prize led to the democratization of air travel and accelerated a period of expansion that would last until the start of WWII. The period would later become known as aviation's "Golden Age."

The Orteig prize created a culture of competition that propelled nine teams to challenge Earth's second largest ocean. By conquering the Atlantic, Lindbergh liberated the masses tethered by invisible ties to the ground. His exploits inspired passion and cultural change.

From WWII until the 1970s, the aviation industry continued to blossom. In this post war period, mankind achieved amazing aeronautical advances. In 1947, mankind went supersonic when Chuck Yeager blasted the Bell X-1 through the sound barrier. In 1961, man conquered the sky when Russian cosmonaut Yuri Gagurin became the first human to reach outer space and orbit the Earth. Then, on July 20, 1969, humanity achieved perhaps its greatest achievement when Neil Armstrong and Buzz Aldrin piloted the Eagle lunar lander onto the Moon's surface touching down in the Sea of Tranquility.

Rapid technological advances combined with proliferation of the turbine engine revolutionized commercial travel. People could now travel virtually anywhere on the globe at a pace and a cost that previous generations would have considered unimaginable. This transformation spurred globalization and drove tremendous economic growth and social change around the world.

But since 1972, no human has visited the moon. The Cold War tensions between the US and the Soviets that fueled the Space Race waned in the late 1980s. While the world became a safer place to live, space became a place far less explored.

Established by Eisenhower and propelled by Kennedy, NASA once zealously pushed the boundaries of space with the unwavering support of the US government cheered on by the US citizenry. Over time, the support and drive of NASA slowly atrophied. No single blow signaled the end for NASA. A series of events slowly debilitated the once proud civilian space program.

The US defeated the Russians in the Cold War. Capitalism triumphed over the Evil Empire. And, as a result, NASA's progress no longer represented a strategic national imperative. Two disastrous crashes, the Challenger in 1986 and Columbia in 2003, shook public support. The US government's burgeoning debt exacerbated the problem. Government bloat, lack of galvanizing purpose, and limited public support all combined to cripple NASA.

NASA, once a cutting-edge innovator, had broken few milestones since the Apollo Program. The Space Shuttle program and International Space Station gave NASA some purpose in decades following Apollo. But NASA didn't make more manned trips to the moon. No other government or agency made a manned trip to Mars or any other planet. The final frontier of Space had been pushed no further.

NASA, buoyed by President Kennedy's great zag, achieved one of mankind's greatest accomplishments. Decades later, unable to push the final frontier further, NASA was forced to shutter its Space Shuttle Program in 2011. Mankind had made only small steps, no giant leaps since the 1970s.

Over half a century later, in the early 1990s, an entrepreneur named Peter Diamandis read Charles Lindbergh's book *The Spirit of St. Louis*. Like many, Diamandis was not impressed by NASA's efforts since

Apollo: "I don't think the space station is innovative. Going to the moon was innovative because we had no idea how to do it."

Unimpressed by NASA and inspired by Orteig, Diamandis set out to change the future of space flight. To accomplish his goal, he followed Orteig's lead and created a culture of competition.

Symbolically, Diamandis returned to Lindbergh's hometown of St. Louis to commence his challenge. There he announced the largest such prize in world history – $10 million to the first team who could place a three-man crew 100 kilometers into space twice in three weeks.

Similar to what Orteig experienced, Diamandis' competition, later branded the Ansari X PRIZE for Suborbital Spaceflight, attracted cumulative investment that greatly exceeded the value of the prize.

Collectively, 26 teams invested over $100 million dollars. And it took only eight years for the team funded by Microsoft co-founder Paul Allen and led by legendary aerospace engineer Burt Rutan to claim the prize.*

Space flight was no longer a failed government monopoly. A new industry of commercial spaceflight was born. While still in its infancy, the future is extremely promising. Since the prize was awarded, over $1.5 billion dollars has been invested to develop the private spaceflight industry. Technology has advanced. And mankind no

---

* Rutan has had a prolific career. In addition to SpaceShip One the winner of the Anasari X Prize, he also designed the Virgin Atlantic GlobalFlyer which set the world record for fastest circumnavigation of the Earth and Voyager which was the first aircraft to circle the Earth without refueling.

longer requires government to push the frontier further into the cosmos.

Encouraged by the success of the Anasari X prize, Diamandis' X Prize Foundation created more competitions like the Progressive Insurance Automotive X PRIZE. This prize was established for developing a super fuel efficient vehicle that could achieve over 100 miles per gallon (MPGe) with minimal carbon emissions. 111 teams representing 10 countries entered the competition. Three teams eventually split the prize, each achieving goals in different sub-categories of the competition.

Additionally, prizes have been created in the areas of Genomics, Life Sciences, Energy and the Environment, and Exploration. Teams from around the world currently pursue prizes in diverse and important pursuits such as rapid genome sequencing and accelerating the cleanup of oil spills. Mankind is making progress in many areas, all spurred on by the spirit of competition.

The largest prize is the $30 million Google Lunar X Prize. Diamandis' X Prize Foundation will award the prize to the privately funded team that successfully lands a robot on the moon, travels more than 500 meters, and transmits high resolution images back to Earth. The team who accomplishes this first will win $20 million. The second team will claim $5 million. Teams can earn additional smaller prizes for traveling further on the moon's surface or capturing images of remnants from the Apollo missions.

The X Prize foundation explains their philosophy: "We believe in the power of competition. That it's part of our DNA. Of humanity, itself. That tapping into that indomitable spirit of competition brings about breakthroughs and solutions that once seemed unimaginable. Impossible."

By creating a culture of competition, mankind created greatness when conventional approaches had faltered. Dr. Buzz Aldrin, the NASA astronaut who joined Neil Armstrong on the Apollo 11 moon mission riffed on his former partner's most famous line: "I think the [Ansari] X PRIZE should be viewed as the beginning of one giant leap."

CHAPTER 27

ROSA AND THE REST OF THE STORY

"A genuine leader is not a searcher for consensus but a molder of consensus."

"Change does not roll in on the wheels of inevitability, but comes through continuous struggle. And so, we must straighten our backs and work for our freedom. A man can't ride you unless your back is bent."

– Martin Luther King Jr.

Most know the story about Rosa Parks, the department store seamstress whose bravery accelerated the civil rights movement in the United States. But the story taught in elementary schools only tells part of the story.

Prior to the Civil Rights Movement, in the Deep South, Jim Crow laws enforced racial segregation. Blacks were forced to attend different schools, use different restrooms, and drink from separate water fountains than whites.

Among these and many other grave injustices, blacks had to sit at the back of public busses and yield their seats to white passengers when ordered to move.

In the traditional telling of the story, Rosa Parks, tired from a long day of work, took a seat on a Montgomery, Alabama bus in the front of the "Colored Section." When the bus began to fill, the driver ordered Rosa Parks and three other African Americans to move to the back to make room for white passengers.

On December 1, 1955, when the bus driver asked Rosa to give up her seat and move to the back, he expected her to comply quickly and without issue. When she refused to yield, the driver had her arrested.

A few days later, on December 5th, Parks had her trial. The court found her guilty and fined her $10 plus $4 in court costs. That same day, African Americans across Montgomery led by a young minister named Martin Luther King Jr. and his best friend and fellow minster Ralph Abernathy started a boycott of Montgomery's busses that would last an incredible 381 days.

During the protracted protest, segregationists tried everything to stop the nascent Civil Rights Movement. They bombed churches. They bombed the houses of King and Abernathy. But, through it all, the boycotters remained steadfast in their resolve.

While the boycott continued, Parks' case worked its way through the legal system. As plaintiff, she challenged that segregated busses violated the 14th amendment to the Constitution that guarantees all citizens, regardless of race, equal protection under the law.

By June, the Montgomery Federal court ruled in her favor. But the City of Montgomery appealed sending the case to the US Supreme Court.

On December 20, 1956, a little over a year after Rosa Parks refused to give up her seat, the US Supreme Court ruled in her favor. The next day, Montgomery integrated its bus system. Rosa Parks had won.

In the traditional telling of the story, Rosa Parks' brave act served as the catalyst, and a couple of opportunistic ministers took advantage of the situation to stage a boycott. Thousands of others acted with bravery and incredible resolve, and after a long and arduous fight, they prevailed. Because of their brave actions, they changed society for the better. They fought long and hard and eventually broke free from the shackles of the culture that oppressed them.

Every single one of these facts is true. But this telling of the story doesn't give Parks or King the credit they truly deserve. It also doesn't give appropriate credit to E.D. Nixon and Jo Ann Robinson. All of these people acted with courage, but they didn't make extemporaneous decisions. Their decisions were carefully calculated and made with the expectation of success.

In the traditional telling, Rosa Parks was simply tired. And on the spur of the moment, decided to stay seated and not move to the back of the bus. But that's not entirely true.

Rosa Parks and her husband Raymond Parks were long-time active members of the National Association for the Advancement of Colored People (NAACP). This organization promoted equal rights for all people and fought to eradicate racism. It was one of the most important Civil Rights organizations in the country.

In December 1943, Rosa Parks became Secretary of the Montgomery chapter of the NAACP – a position she still held 12 years later on the day she refused to yield her seat.

And December 1, 1955 wasn't the first-time Rosa Parks made a protest on a bus. Twelve years earlier, she refused to comply with a rule that required black passengers to pay their fare, then exit the bus, and reenter through the back door. Amazingly, the bus driver on that day was James Blake – the same bus driver who had Rosa Parks arrested in 1955.

In her autobiography, Rosa Parks corrects the apocryphal claim that she was simply tired. Parks clarifies, "People always say that I didn't give up my seat because I was tired, but that isn't true. I was not tired physically… No, the only tired I was, was tired of giving in."

Rosa Parks wasn't just a tired seamstress who made a spur of the moment decision to protest. She was an educated, strong, proud, long-time leader of a Civil Rights organization with a history of non-violent protest who made a mindful decision to protest the segregation laws she had worked against for decades.

During her work with the NAACP, Rosa Parks worked closely with the Chapter President, a man named E.D. Nixon. Nixon would eventually become one of the most important figures in the Civil Rights movement. During this tumultuous time, Nixon formed a critical partnership with Jo Ann Robison, President of the Women's Political

Council, an organization of African-American female professionals.

In the early 1950s, Nixon and Robinson decided to challenge the segregation laws on the grounds that they were unconstitutional. But they needed to find the perfect case and the perfect plaintiff to achieve success. They planned and they waited.

Nixon had opportunities before the Parks case, but he passed. He decided to pass on one woman because he didn't think she could endure the lengthy process. He passed on another because of allegations that her father drank too much. He passed on Claudette Colvin, who 9 months before Parks, refused to yield her seat on a bus because Colvin, just 15 at the time, was pregnant.

Nixon needed the perfect plaintiff – courageous and strong with unquestioned integrity. He got his wish with Rosa Parks.

After Park's arrest, she called her husband to bail her out of jail. By the time the authorities released her that evening, E.D. Nixon had already arrived at the courthouse. Later, Nixon met with Parks, her mom, and her husband and convinced them that Parks could challenge segregation and win.

Nixon's decision to challenge Jim Crow with the Parks' case wasn't haphazard. It was calculated and years in the making. Nixon was just waiting for the perfect case and the perfect plaintiff. When he found them and expected success, he made his move.

Nixon and the others did make a quick decision to boycott the Montgomery bus system, but the civil rights leaders had an organized plan that they executed with the great efficiency.

Jo Ann Robinson leveraged her well organized Women's Political Council to quickly spread the word. A well-connected group of black ministers shared the plan with their congregations. And the Montgomery Advertiser newspaper published a full-page article detailing the boycott.

The results exceeded all expectations. 40,000 African Americans boycotted the next morning. To capitalize on the momentum, the opportunistic leaders met later that day and created the Montgomery Improvement Association. They elected a young, little-known Minister named Martin Luther King Jr. as President and decided to continue the boycott until the city met their demands.

Clearly, the leadership recognized something special in King. But they also elected him because he was new to the area, relatively unknown, and hadn't created too many enemies yet – another carefully considered and calculated decision made with the expectation of success.

The boycott endured for 381 days. It withstood not just because of the passion and will of the people, but because of the well-organized, effective, and coordinated leadership across several key people and groups. The social network stitched together by church and civic leaders mobilized and energized an army for a protracted battle. They organized car pools and black taxi-drivers provided transport for the same cost as a bus ride. Leaders held meetings to keep the troops informed, organized, and motivated in the face of violent opposition.

The traditional telling of the story is a wonderful story of bravery and resilience. It is a remarkable story of enduring struggle and ultimate victory. But the full story is even more amazing and wonderful.

Rosa wasn't just a random, tired seamstress. She was selected as the perfect plaintiff. The boycotts weren't just a display of bravery and endurance. They were an incredible execution of a well-crafted strategy planned and led by remarkable elected leaders and highly capable organizations.

Those 381 days forever changed the culture of the United States for the better. Their actions accelerated a Civil Rights Movement that would quickly spread across the United States and forever improve the culture of the country.

The segregationists expected the African Americans of Montgomery to act like compliant little sardines and stay neatly in their shoal. But they refused. They broke free. And while brave, their actions weren't foolhardy. They were bold, calculated decisions to break free made with the expectation of success. They planned, they waited, and when the opportunity presented itself, they zagged.

Post Script

Civil Rights Movement leaders like Martin Luther King Jr. fought to end the practice of segregation in the American South to ensure that all people, regardless of skin color, received the same rights and protections. Nelson Mandela led a similar movement against Apartheid, the system of legal racial segregation in South Africa.

A long time before both King and Mandela, President Abraham Lincoln issued an executive order known as the Emancipation Proclamation abolishing the practice of slavery in the American South. The Proclamation made abolition a central focus of the US Civil War paving the way for eradication of slavery in the United States via the 13th Amendment to the US Constitution.

Numerous women's right movements have transpired over the centuries inspired and championed by a wide variety of people and groups. Early stoic philosophers advocated for gender equality in ancient Greece and Rome. Later, Susan B. Anthony and Elizabeth Cady Stanton in the United States, Emmeline Pankhurst in Great Britain, and many others around the globe led successful women's suffrage movements.

Around the world and over the years, countless others have zagged and driven cultural change – Lech Walesa, Gandhi, Pope John Paul II, the Dalai Lama, the list goes on and on. Many are famous, and many are not. Regardless, they have one thing in common. They weren't bound by the societal conventions of their time. They challenged convention, blazed a different trail, and changed a culture.

These trailblazers led counter-cultural movements that challenged long-held conventional beliefs and behaviors and created new norms. While the multitudes who came before them simply swam along unaware or unwilling to fight for positive change, these brave leaders made the conscious decision to break from cultural convention and change society for the better. Where others zigged, they zagged.

Their accomplishments are so impressive because culture is so powerful. By defining the relationships between people, culture creates an environment that suppresses individual thought. In this way, culture can prove limiting, even dangerous.

Culture's pervasive impact affects each of us, every day. Slowly but surely easing us into the same grooves travelled by other members of our group. Over time, those grooves grow deeper. Before too long, our paths are predetermined. And we find it increasingly difficult to break free, to think differently, and to zag.

Milgram postulated that awareness is the first step to liberating us from our cultural tendencies: "It may be that we are puppets-puppets controlled by the strings of society. But at least we are puppets with perception, with awareness. And perhaps our awareness is the first step to our liberation."

According to Milgram, emancipation from culture begins with understanding our true predicament. To break free from the shackles of culture, one must realize that he or she is enslaved in the first place.

We may be puppets. But we are puppets who can choose to break free and zag.

Part Five

Information

CHAPTER 28

MURKY WATER

"The bulk of the world's knowledge is an imaginary construction. We differ, blind and seeing, one from another, not in our senses, but in the use, we make of them, in the imagination and courage with which we seek wisdom beyond the senses."

– Hellen Keller

Most have heard the parable of the blind men and the elephant. Philosophers, teachers, and religious leaders have used the story in a variety of ways to illustrate points about relativism and the importance of perspective.

In one of the earlier and most famous versions of the story, Buddha describes the actions of a wise king who summons blind men to his palace and instructs them to touch an elephant and describe the animal. One man touches the foot and believes the elephant to be like a pillar. One man touches the tip of the tail and thinks the elephant is like a brush. Others touch the ear, the tusk, the body and all get widely different impressions of the same animal. With limited information, each blind man fails to truly comprehend the elephant in its entirety.

They are all wrong, limited in their knowledge, blinded by their limited perspective. Yet, they are all convinced that they know the true elephant. They cleave to their beliefs based on their limited information, certain that they are the one who knows the true elephant. Eventually, the blind men fight over who is right.

Buddha compares these feuding blind men to preachers and teachers so limited in their view yet so convicted in their beliefs:

> *O how they cling and wrangle, some who claim*
> *For preacher and monk, the honored name!*
> *For, quarreling, each to his view they cling.*
> *Such folk see only one side of a thing.*

The parable illuminates the power of information. The information available influences the way one understands reality, interprets situations, and therefore, determines how one acts in the world. Like the blind men, people cling to the information they have and act consistently with that information. The problem is that the information is often severely limited or interpreted in a biased way. And sometimes, the available information is completely wrong.

Consider the case of the Titanic, the unsinkable ocean liner that unexpectedly sank on her maiden voyage. Before embarking, Captain Smith, Commander of Titanic infamously proclaimed: "I cannot imagine any condition which would cause a ship to founder. I cannot conceive of any vital disaster happening to this vessel. Modern ship building has gone beyond that."

This erroneous information led to tragic results. Believing in the infallibility of their vessel, the crew failed to issue binoculars to lookout Frederick Fleet. Had Fleet spotted the blue iceberg a little bit earlier, the Captain could have veered sooner and circumnavigated the massive obstacle. Had they recognized the potential for disaster, they might have equipped the vessel with enough lifeboats to hold all the passengers and trained the crew on how to evacuate the ship.

They didn't make either preparation. The lifeboats had space for only about half of those on board and the improperly trained crew launched many boats at less than half capacity. The Captain and crew squandered many lives because of a terrible assumption grounded in flawed information. No one thought it could sink. No one prepared. Everyone acted the same way. The results were tragic.

Sometimes people have incorrect information like the Captain and Crew of the Titanic. They are like the sardine who joins the great shoal on its northern migration headlong into a death trap, clueless to the danger that lies ahead.

Oftentimes people have incomplete information like the blind monks with the elephant. These people focus narrowly on limited portions of the data blinded by their tunnel vision. Often, they will make rational choices, but those decisions are bounded by their limited perspective.

Sometimes people have access to all the necessary information. Even then, they can interpret it with bias. As humans, we tend to share the same biases, and as a result, the same flawed interpretations leading to conventional decisions and failed outcomes.

Typically, this isn't a problem. Commonly held information is frequently good enough to enable reasonably effective decision making and produce good results. But commonly held information interpreted commonly will never produce great results.

To zag, one must acquire new information or use it in a novel way. In the dark, cloudy waters of murky information, most just zig along in the shoal. A rare few zag and achieve greatness.

CHAPTER 29

THIN SLICE

"There can be as much value in the blink of an eye as in months of rational analysis."

– Malcolm Gladwell, *Blink*

:-)　　　　　;-)　　　　:-(
Smiley face.　Winking at you.　Sad face.

Our brain is amazing. From just a quick glimpse at a few symbols, it can discern expression. Faces with emotion arise from carefully placed colons, semicolons, and parentheses.

This amazing capability is an ingrained, evolutionary adaptation of our species. Instantly and without conscious thought, our brains recognize meaning with only limited information.

Let's try another test of our incredible cognitive capabilities.

INFORMATION

Do either of these famous images look familiar?

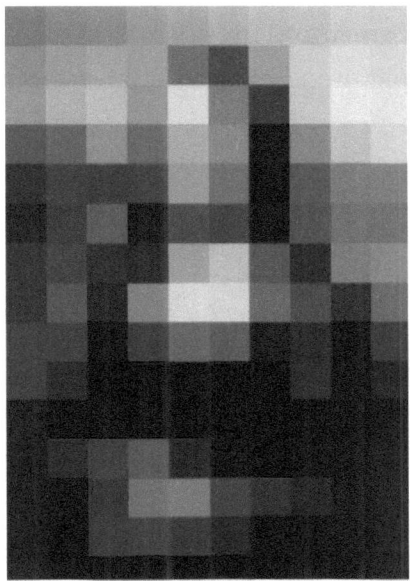

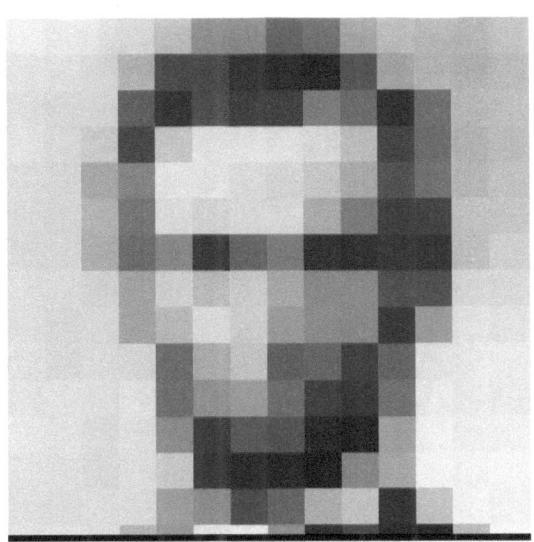

Despite having been degraded to just 12x14 pixels of color, most can recognize these famous faces. The Mona Lisa with her faint smile and president Lincoln with his stoic countenance are pictured below in full resolution.

If you couldn't identify the degraded visages the first time, flip back and try again. After exposure to the full resolution image, you should have no trouble seeing the Mona Lisa and President Lincoln in the degraded images.*

In 1992, psychologists Nalini Ambady and Robert Rosenthal coined the term "thin slicing" to describe human's amazing ability to understand and find patterns based on just "thin-slices" of experience. Later in 2005, this concept gained widespread awareness when renowned author Malcolm Gladwell penned his best-seller *Blink*.

In *Blink*, Gladwell argues that what people feel as intuition is really the outcome of an amazing unconscious process. People rapidly process information, quickly and frugally parse the available data, reconcile it with past experiences, and make decisions in the blink of an eye. Gladwell cites numerous examples where the unconscious mind, with minimal deliberation, makes remarkably accurate predictions. Many times, the predictions made "in the blink of an eye" prove better than those made following months of deliberate and rational analysis.

Gladwell starts his book with the story of the Getty Kouros, a purportedly 2,500-year-old Greek Statue, later proved to be a fraud. While extensive scientific tests were unable to confirm the authenticity of the Kouros, an individual expert in the field, was able to take one quick look at the statue and know it was a fraud. In the blink of

---

* Dr. Pawan Sinha, an MIT professor and a leading researcher in the area of visual cognition, found that 75% of test subjects could correctly identify faces with just 12x14 pixels of information. The amazing mind needs just a tiny bit of information to discern meaning and correctly identify a person.

an eye, an expert's trained and experienced adaptive unconscious mind accomplished what weeks of rigorous testing failed to achieve.

Gladwell continues to detail other examples of this amazing ability of the human mind. He details the story of John Gottman, a marital counselor with an amazing ability to predict the success of a relationship. Based on his experience in the field and just one hour of conversation with a couple, Gottman can predict with 95% accuracy if that couple will be married in 15 years. Amazingly, with more information gathered during a two-hour long conversation, his accuracy rate dips to 90%.

While the term "thin-slicing" has only been around for a few decades, the notion that the brain processes information quickly and holistically has been around for well over a century. Gestalt psychology posits that the brain organizes things holistically rather than as the sum of individual parts. Gestalt theorists such as Max Wertheimer, Kurt Koffka, and Wolfgang Köhler would argue that people don't view the world as a series of individual pieces and elements. Instead, humans seamlessly process individual bits of information and organize them into meaningful and unified wholes.

Gestalt theory adds an interesting layer of interpretation to the examples offered by Gladwell in *Blink*. While the scientists who tested the Getty Kouros examined specific elements of the statue such as its color, density, and composition, the art expert saw it holistically and deduced that it was a fraud. While traditional methods of predicting the success of a marriage would hinge on extensive personality surveys and compatibility tests, Gottman takes in the totality of the relationship via normal conversation and creates extraordinarily accurate predictions.

Where traditional rational analysis tries to make sense of the world by evaluating the individual parts of a complex whole, the human mind naturally and subconsciously takes a holistic approach. This way of processing coupled with individual expertise gives the approach taken by the art expert and Gottman a leg up on traditional rational analysis.

People don't experience the world as a sum of parts, they see it as meaningful wholes. To gain an appreciation for how this phenomenon works, take a look at the image below. What do you see?

If it's your first time viewing this image, you will probably only notice a bunch of white and black spots with no discernible image.

Now try again, but this time with some help.

With the help of the outline, one can see a Dalmatian.

Now, flip back to the previous page to the image without the outline. Do you see the dog?

Most will see the dog now, and if they look back at this image a year from now, they will still see the dog. Once the learning has occurred and the brain has been able to organize the disparate spots into a cohesive whole, the brain's self-organizing nature will continue to see the order among the chaos.

The Dalmatian is now a whole construct. The brain couldn't perceive the Dalmatian as a series of parts and then formulate a whole dog. The brain first needed to perceive the dog as a whole before being able to make sense of the chaotic scene.

In the Dalmatian example, there is an actual dog in the disorderly image, and our brain, with a little assistance, successfully organizes and makes sense of the chaos. However, sometimes our brain, in an effort to organize and make sense of the world, sees things when they don't actually exist.

The following image, known as the Kanizsa Triangle, provides an example of how this works.

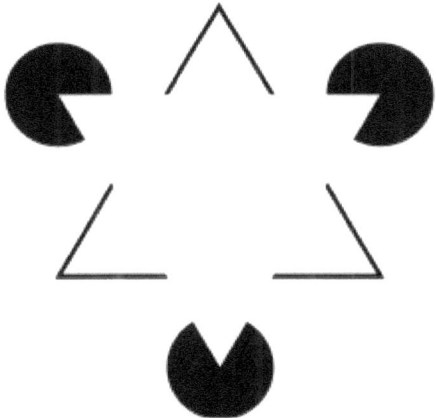

Do you see the white triangle? Do you see the black outline of a triangle? Most do. They see a white triangle and a black triangle outline resting on top of three black circles. In reality, there are no triangles and there are no black circles. In an effort to organize the world and interpret it holistically, the brain perceives these shapes when they don't exist.

This phenomenon is known as reification and is a key principle in Gestalt. Here are a few more reification examples.

In this one, most perceive a three-dimensional sphere.

In these images, known as Ehrenstein illusions, most perceive bright disks among the straight lines.

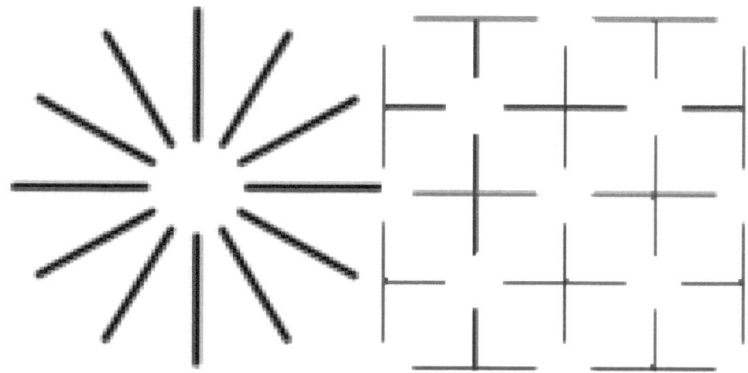

But there is no three-dimensional sphere. There are no bright disks. In an effort to organize the world, the brain sometimes perceives objects and patterns that don't exist.

INFORMATION

The brain processes stimuli, not as a sum of parts, but as holistic constructs. This happens not just with images, but with other forms of visual processing as well. In the paragraph below, virtually every word is misspelled, but most don't have a problem reading the text and understanding it completely.

Aoccdrnig to a rscheearch at Cmabrigde Uinervtisy, it deosn't mttaer in waht oredr the ltteers in a wrod are, the olny iprmoetnt tihng is taht the frist and lsat ltteer be at the rghit pclae. The rset can be a total mses and you can sitll raed it wouthit porbelm. Tihs is bcuseae the huamn mnid deos not raed ervey lteter by istlef, but the wrod as a wlohe.

The amazing mind quickly and efficiently processes the garbled information in the paragraph above with little difficulty. To the mind, the paragraph is not just a collection of letters to be individually processed and added up to find meaning. Rather, the mind interprets words as wholes and doesn't let a few misplaced letters get in the way.

The mind processes the words similarly to the way it locates the Dalmatian in the chaos and sees the Kanizsa Triangle when no three-sided object exists. The mind quickly and efficiently processes incomplete information. It seamlessly unifies the world into meaningful wholes. And it does it without need or regard for many of the details.

Most of the time, this method of quick and efficient processing works very well. But sometimes it results in mistakes.

In its haste to efficiently digest and process data, the brain frequently misses critical information. To demonstrate, please read the following sentence and count the number of "Fs" that appear in the text.

FINISHED FILES ARE THE RESULT OF YEARS OF SCIENTIFIC STUDY

COMBINED WITH THE EXPERIENCE OF YEARS

How many "F's" did you count?

Most people count 3 or 4, but in fact, there are 6. If you didn't find all 6, please try again before flipping to the next page.

All 6 "F's" are highlighted below:

FINISHED **F**ILES ARE THE RESULT O**F** YEARS O**F** SCIENTI**F**IC STUDY

COMBINED WITH THE EXPERIENCE O**F** YEARS

Most won't be able to find the 6 "Fs" despite their best efforts. It's an incredibly straightforward task – a simple counting of letters. It's a task where preschoolers tend to outperform older, more educated people. But why?

In a quick reading, the brain focuses on the words that are most important to the meaning of the sentence and only pays cursory attention to the less significant grammatical functions like conjunctions and articles. The brain more thoroughly processes the lexical words such as "Finished" and "Files" while skimming over words such as "Of" and "With."

Understandably, this phenomenon is accentuated in advanced readers. While an illiterate preschooler would mundanely and correctly count the "Fs" among a seemingly meaningless collection of text, the advanced reader would efficiently process the words as wholes and quickly construct a meaningful sentence. The advanced reader quickly processes the text, but they miss critical information relative to the task at hand.

In addition to missing critical information, people have the tendency to see meaningful patterns where there is none. Psychologists call this phenomenon pareidolia. When confronted with vague stimuli, the brain instinctively searches for patterns and whole constructs that make sense of the clutter.

Take for example this satellite image from Google Maps of an area outside of Medicine Hat, Alberta, Canada:

Is this a Native American with an iPod?

What about this image of a mesa in the Cydonia region of Mars captured by the Viking 1 orbiter?

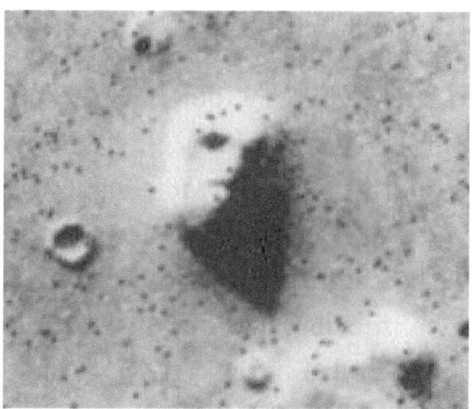

Is this a face on Mars?

How about this Google Maps image of "The dinosaur lake" in Zagreb, Croatia?

People find faces of Jesus or the Virgin Mary on tortillas. People see clouds that look positively like spaceships, animals, and people. African Mahogany trees calloused by trauma take on the appearance of monkeys, cinnamon buns bear an eerie resemblance to Mother Theresa, and the visage of Barak Obama emerges on a grilled Cheese sandwich.

People usually do an amazing job of quickly and efficiently operating with just the thinnest slices of information. They seamlessly process stimuli as unified and meaningful wholes to enable cognition and decision making. They do it so quickly and effortlessly that it appears as intuition. But it is not intuition at all. It is rapid cognition enabled by the highly evolved and miraculous human mind.

But the miraculous mind can make mistakes. In our haste to make quick decisions, we sometimes neglect to notice critical information. Sometimes we see things that don't exist. And sometimes we see patterns when there is only a burnt sandwich.

CHAPTER 30

DROWNING IN DATA

"To know the true reality of yourself, you must be aware not only of your conscious thoughts, but also of your unconscious prejudices, bias and habits."

– Anonymous

The brain is amazing, but it does have its limits. When the mind efficiently leaps to unify a complex world into meaningful wholes, it often misses critical pieces of information, fills in the blanks with imaginary objects, or constructs artificial patterns from randomness.

In these cases, the human mind's amazing ability to efficiently operate with limited data turns from a blessing into a curse. Groups of people, usually adept at dealing with incomplete and incorrect information, make similar mental leaps and commit similar mistakes. They all see the same Native American with the iPod, infer the same Kanizsa Triangle, or skim over the same Fs. They all take the same leap and fail.

But we don't just encounter small, thin slices of information. Our environment continually bombards us with a barrage of data. To put it into perspective, humans currently create as much information every two days as humanity created from the dawn of civilization up until 2003. This incredible volume stretches the human mind and its ability to make decisions to the breaking point.

Similar to how people handle limited data, humans possess a tremendous ability to cope with large quantities of information. To manage the deluge, people have developed a series of mental shortcuts known as heuristics. These practical approaches enable us to quickly find satisfactory solutions to the problems we encounter every day.

Heuristics help people make good decisions without having to process all the information or think too long to devise a reasonable solution. Heuristics are essential, especially in this complex world flooded with an ocean of data. These mental shortcuts help us avoid drowning, but they predispose people to committing similar mistakes and suffering from the same biases.

The earlier section on mental inertia examined "anchoring." With this common heuristic, people place a premium on the first information received. This creates great efficiency and usually produces satisfactory decisions. By paying attention to the first bit of information, people can avoid completely parsing every last bit of subsequent information. The anchoring heuristic creates great efficiency, but it can bias future thinking.

Anchoring isn't the only coping method humans have developed. To help demonstrate another method, please take the following brief quiz. The following questions are based on deaths that occurred in the United States in 2013.*

1. Do more people die from Assault (Homicide) or Intentional Self Harm (Suicide)?
2. Do more people die from getting shot (Homicide by Firearm) or shooting themselves (Suicide by Firearm)?
3. Do more people die from Auto Accidents or Flu/Pneumonia?
4. Do more people die from Drugs & Alcohol or Diabetes?

The way people tend to answer demonstrates another powerful heuristic. When trying to evaluate a choice, the mind often relies on the most accessible information available to inform that decision. The brain more easily recalls recently received and dramatic information. It also recollects events with large consequences more easily than mundane experiences.

Psychologists refer to this as the "availability heuristic." This mental shortcut helps increase efficiency significantly. When making a choice, the mind doesn't need to fully review every relevant piece of stored memory. It quickly pulls in the most "available" information and usually makes a satisfactory choice.

The availability heuristic proves extremely valuable in a data drenched world. But because of the way we process

---

* National Vital Statistics Reports, Volume 64, Number 2, 2/16/2016.

information, people tend to make the same mistakes. We tend to overweight recent and dramatic information leading to the same, predictable biases.

Since you are smart and you are reading a chapter about heuristics and biases, you may have adjusted your answers on the quiz in anticipation. But when making everyday decisions, people don't adjust. To understand how the availability heuristic leads to biases let's review the answers to the brief quiz.

1. Do more people die from Assault (Homicide) or Intentional Self Harm (Suicide)?

<u>Suicide</u>: In 2013, Suicide (41,149) greatly outnumbered Homicide (16,121) by a factor of 2.5 to 1.

Despite their lower incidence rates, homicides dominate the news. Mass shootings and murders get the headlines. Tragic and horrific scenes burn into people's memories. On the other hand, suicides don't usually make the news. Most families attempt to discretely move on following a loved one's suicide without drawing extra attention. As a result, vivid and well-publicized memories of murders quickly jump to mind skewing the average person's probability assessment.

2. Do more people die from getting shot (Homicide by Firearm) or from shooting themselves (Suicide by Firearm)?

Suicide by Firearm: Suicide by Firearm (21,175) outnumbered Homicide by Firearm (11,208) by nearly 2-1. Again, horrific murder scenes emblazoned into our memory make for easy recall and skewed judgment.

3. Do more people die from Motor Vehicle Accidents or Flu/Pneumonia?

Flu: Flu deaths (56,979) exceeded death by Motor Vehicle Accidents (35,369) by over 60%. Influenza/Pneumonia ranked as the 8th leading cause of death in the United States in 2013. But despite flu's prevalence, the flashing police and ambulance sirens from the last traffic accident you passed on the highway leave an indelible mark.

4. Do more people die from Drugs & Alcohol or Diabetes?

Diabetes: Deaths from Diabetes (75,578) exceeded the deaths from Drug (46,471) and Alcohol (29,001) combined (75,472). Despite being the 7th leading cause of death in the United States, the metabolic disease gets considerably less attention than drug and alcohol deaths that frequent the news cycle and the political and social zeitgeist.

If you got some questions wrong, don't be too concerned. You are not alone. Most people overestimate the probability of well-publicized and dramatic events like tornadoes, motor vehicle accidents, and homicides. While, on the other hand, people tend to underestimate the probability of less-publicized and unsensational events such as asthma, diabetes, and stroke.

In one study, student respondents estimated that death by accident was 25 times more likely than death by stroke.* When in fact, at the time of the study, death by stroke was 85% more likely. Additionally, students believed death by tornado to be a more common killer than asthma, despite asthma being 20 times more likely. Overall, the more dramatic and well-publicized an event, the more frequently people tend to think it actually occurs.

Consider airplane crashes. Most have heard statistics that evidence the incredibly high safety level of air travel. Depending on which statistician you ask, the odds of being killed in a single airline flight range from approximately 1 in 11 million to 30 million.

Yet, people still get nervous when flying. A pit develops in their stomach and they imagine terrible things. They fear scenarios like the ones they have watched in horror on the news. But those terrible things are unbelievably rare and extremely unlikely to happen.

When planes do have accidents, the most common cause is pilot error (53%) followed by mechanical failure (20%) followed by weather (12%). Only 8% of crashes are caused by sabotage.

---

* *"Judged Frequency of Lethal Events"* Lichtenstein et el.

And despite what most think, when planes crash, most people survive.* When looking at commercial airline crashes over a long period of time, over 95% of people survive. Even when looking at just the worst accidents that had at least one death, the survival rate exceeds 75%.

Yet, people are still afraid. The vivid memories of terrible tragedies quickly come to mind. Sensational and dramatic events occupy prime real estate in our brain making them more "available" and readily accessible.

When people avoid flying or worry more about getting bit by a shark than managing their diabetes, they have succumbed to faulty logic. Dramatic events like plane crashes and shark attacks quickly spring to mind skewing the way people assess the risk of swimming in the ocean versus consuming a sugar-laden jelly donut.

When confronted by oceans of information, people need heuristics to make quick decisions. These mental rules of thumb keep us from drowning, but they tend to bias thinking in predictable ways. As humans, we share these mental shortcuts and their wonderful efficiencies. But we also share the resulting biases and shortcomings.

---

* National Transportation Safety Board data from 1983-2000. 95.7% survived commercial airlines. 76.6% survivor rate in crashes with at least one fatality.

CHAPTER 31

OPERATION BODYGUARD

"In wartime, truth is so precious that she should always be attended by a bodyguard of lies."

— Winston Churchill

In war, having correct information is a life and death proposition. The side that knows the truth about the enemy's strengths and weaknesses and the strategies and tactics they will employ has a decided advantage. Through the millennia, the greatest generals have understood the importance of acquiring intelligence about the enemy and about concealing and manipulating their own troop's conditions and battle plans. Never in the course of human history did so much ride on the outcome of a war, and perhaps, never was there a deception plan as extensive as Operation Bodyguard.

World War II was the most widespread and deadliest conflict in world history. From 1939 to 1945, more than 100 million military personnel were mobilized and between 50 and 70 million people lost their lives. The War extended across the entire globe as nations placed their entire economic and industrial capabilities in service of the all-consuming war effort. The fate of the entire world hung in the balance.

In early June 1944, the outcome was very much in doubt. The Axis powers, led by Germany, controlled the majority of Western Europe including France. Germany hadn't surrendered France since capturing the prize four years earlier in what German Führer Adolf Hitler considered "the most famous victory in history."

In 1942, British Prime Minister Winston Churchill, Soviet Premier Joseph Stalin, and United States President Franklin D. Roosevelt all agreed that they needed to establish a second front in Europe to defeat the German forces. The exact location and method for securing a foothold in Western Europe, however, was still very much up for debate. The Allies eventually settled on a plan to be executed by the Supreme Commander of the Allied forces in Europe Dwight D. Eisenhower. That plan was Operation Overlord.

The Allies assigned the code name Operation Overlord to the planned invasion at Normandy, France. The Battle of Normandy commenced on June 6, 1944 on D-Day and continued through the end of August culminating with the Liberation of Paris on August 25, 1944. With the victory, the Allied forces successfully established a formidable base in Western Europe. It was a critical turning point in the War, and one that ultimately led to an Allied victory.

Operation Overlord began at Normandy with the largest amphibious invasion in world history. In the first phase, over 24,000 American, British, French, and

Canadian troops manned a 12,000-plane aerial assault. The second phase involved a massive 5,000 ship mission that carried nearly 160,000 troops to a 50 mile stretch of the Normandy coast. On the first day alone, Allied forces suffered over 12,000 fatalities, and by the time Paris had been liberated from Nazi control nearly three months later, 226,386 Allied troops had laid the ultimate sacrifice upon the alter of freedom.

The battle was costly, but essential for the Allies. France was liberated. The Allies established a beachhead in Western Europe from which to advance. Germany would surrender within a year. The largest and deadliest war in human history would soon come to a close.

Behind the success of Operation Overlord and the heroic Normandy invasion was a lesser known and rarely celebrated operation. This operation was the deception plan that enabled the decisive Allied victory at Normandy. This operation, aptly named Operation Bodyguard, was the largest and most widespread deception plan in military history. Its aim – to successfully cloak the true Allied plans in a bodyguard of lies.

Once the Allies settled on Normandy as the target, the Allied command embarked on a cunning disinformation plan. The plan had simple, but critical objectives. Achieving them would be critical to the war effort.

First, the Allies wanted to convince the Germans that the attack would take place somewhere other than Normandy. This would cause the Axis to increase their strength and fortifications in other geographies weakening their defenses close to the intended target. Second, the

Allies wanted the Germans to expect the attack later in the year. This would create the element of surprise. Third, after the initial assault, the Allies wanted to contain and delay the movement of German troops to Normandy for 14 days. This would give the Allies time to defeat the German troops and fortifications and firmly establish a beachhead.

Allied leaders subdivided Operation Bodyguard into 36 smaller operations. The primary ones were Operation Fortitude and Operation Zeppelin.

Operation Fortitude had two components. The Allies designed the northern part to trick the Germans into expecting an invasion in Norway. The southern element aimed to convince the Germans that the real attack would occur at the Pas de Calais, a coastal area in France, close to England with a difficult to defend coastline.

Allied commanders devised Operation Zeppelin to trick the Germans into thinking the attack would occur in Crete, western Greece, or the Romanian Black Sea coast.

To create the illusion of alternate attack points, the Allies employed many techniques. The first technique, and possibly most successful one, is nearly as old as war itself. It involved espionage and the use of double agents.

The British double agent network known as double-cross or XX, a subdivision of MI5, played a critical role. They used double agents to filter carefully constructed false information to the Germans.

As part of the ruse, the Allies completely fabricated a group known as the First United States Army Group (FUSAG). The fictitious Army supposedly stood stationed and assembled in preparation for an attack at the Pas de

Calais. To add to the credibility to the FUSAG, the Allies placed famous and widely regarded General George S. Patten in command. The deception included dummy military vehicles such as inflatable tanks, sea vessels, and even fake uniforms and insignia. The Allies also created fake radio chatter and troop barracks. They shrewdly allowed German spies to photograph them to complete the illusion.

The British spies carefully passed limited pieces of information to the Germans. If they passed along too much, the Germans would get suspicions. To avoid detection and increase credibility, the Allies carefully selected the nuggets they leaked.

The deception worked. The Germans became absolutely convinced of an invasion at the Pas de Calais. Some of the double agents played their roles so convincingly that the Germans awarded them the Iron Cross, a highly-prized German military decoration, for their contributions to the war effort. The illusion worked so well that the Germans retained 15 divisions in the Pas de Calais even after the attacks commenced on D-Day just in case the Normandy landing was just a diversion from the real invasion at the Pas de Calais.

After the D-Day invasion, the Allies continued the ruse to delay Germany's movement of troops and equipment to Normandy. To extend the deception, the Allies executed many smaller operations. In Operation Titanic, the Allies dropped hundreds of dummy parachutists with rifle fire simulators on beach locations away from Normandy. The Allies equipped the apparatus with explosives that would trigger upon landing giving the impression that a paratrooper had landed and simply burned his parachute.

In Operations, Taxable and Glimmer, the Allies used aircraft to drop metal foil chaff known as window near the Pas de Calais. When the German radar scanned the skies, the window created the illusion of a massive invasion. To add to the deceit, the Allies broadcast fake radio chatter that simulated an attack.

They executed these and many other operations as part of carefully constructed bodyguard of lies designed to deceive the Germans. In the end, the Allies' massive deception plan led to victory at Normandy, and ultimately, to victory in the largest and most destructive war in world history. The fate of humanity hung in the balance, and the Allies, with their bravery and cunning, emerged victorious, forever changing the future of the world.

The Germans proved unable to overcome the inaccurate information they received and swam blindly, like sardines, directly into the Allies' trap. They expected an attack at what appeared to be the most logical place, the Pas de Calais. The Germans readily took the Allies' bait and fell hook, line, and sinker for the ruse. Germany zigged.

On the other hand, the Allies used the power of information against their enemy by constructing a brilliant deception plan using misinformation to defeat the Axis. The Allies zagged.

CHAPTER 32

THE BOY WHO LIVED

"We have found the secret of life."

— Francis Crick, Co-Discoverer of DNA and Nobel Prize Recipient

According to popular legend, James D. Watson and Francis Crick walked into a pub in Cambridge England in 1953, and Crick boldly declared, "We have found the secret of life."

The secret Watson and Crick discovered is the correct double helix structure of Deoxyribose Nucleic Acid, or DNA. DNA had been discovered decades earlier and science already understood that it played a critical role in genetics, but not until Watson and Crick did the world fully understand the structure and nature of the molecule. For their discovery and contributions, Watson and Crick were honored with the Nobel Prize in Physiology or Medicine.

Watson and Crick's discovery and their subsequent work marked the genesis of a new field of science known as molecular biology. The discovery of DNA and subsequent developments in molecular biology spawned several important advances.

In forensics, DNA evidence helps put criminals behind bars and helps exonerate those wrongly convicted. In agriculture, genetic engineering has led to more productive and disease resistant crops helping to feed the world's burgeoning population.

In a monumental project known as the Human Genome Project, scientists around the globe worked collaboratively for 13 years to identify the approximately 25,000 genes and sequence the 3 billion chemical base pairs found in human DNA. This work has led to progress against predicting, diagnosing, and treating disease. Because of the Project, scientists will find better ways to treat, manage, and cure various illnesses.

Fast forward from the pub in Cambridge in 1953 to a hospital room in Wisconsin in 2010. Nearly six decades following discovery of the double helix, four-year-old Nicholas Volker suffers from a mysterious bowel malady that has perplexed doctors for the entirety of his young life.

In his first four years, Nic endured over 100 surgeries including the removal of his colon. Nic suffers from a relentless bowel disease of unknown origin. His prognosis is bleak. None of the countless experts who has examined him have been able to identify the cause of his ailment, let alone identify an effective course of treatment.

Nic's parents refused to give up hope. In an effort to save their ailing son, they took Nic to the Medical College of Wisconsin where a team of doctors and researchers have a novel idea. They decide to employ a new gene sequencing technology to map out Nic's genetic code.

This amazing technology sifts through a person's entire genetic code breaking their DNA into manageable chunks. It methodically maps out these chunks into what are known as nucleotide pairs. Researchers can then review the nucleotide pairs for aberrations or mutations.

In these pairs, just four nucleobases Adenine (A), Thymine (T), Guanine (G), and Cytosine (C) carry the entirety of a person's genetic code. These nucleobases attach to each other in a consistent way. A always pairs with T. C always bonds with G. These paired nucleobases then combine with alternating sugars (deoxyribose and phosphate) to form the nucleotide pairs.

Then, just like a binary computer code uses lengthy strings of 0s and 1s to create complex programs, DNA uses the series of A-T and C-G nucleotide pairs to define a person's entire genetic code. In the human genome, these nucleotide pairs number over 3 billion. Segments of the nucleotide pairs combine to make genes which are organized into 23 pairs of chromosomes. The entire string coils together in a beautiful double helix structure resembling a spiral staircase.

In the case of Nicholas Volker, the sequencing technology identified a number of potential mutations for researchers to explore. After some yeoman-like work on the part of Nic's medical team, the search zeroed in on just one mutation in one nucleotide pair. Among Nic's roughly 3.2 billion nucleotide pairs, there was just one that was responsible for his illness.

On the X chromosome, on gene XIAC, the nucleotide combination for every person ever sequenced was T-G-T. For that matter, every single other animal from fruit flies to chickens to cows has a T-G-T sequence at that point of the genetic code.

Not Nic.

Nic's sequence is T-A-T.

In a series of over 3 billion, there was just one mistake. Where there should have been a G, there was an A. Because of this one seemingly small mistake – a tiny misprint, Nic's body produces a different amino acid than it should. This puts his immune system in a constant struggle with his intestinal tract.

This was literally a one in 3 billion discovery.

The discovery also suggested a different course of treatment – a bone marrow transplant. At the age of 5, Nic was scheduled for the risky surgery, but due to complications from the disease that had ravaged and weakened his body, doctors pursued an alternative treatment. They opted to transplant umbilical cord blood from a donor.

The transplant would effectively give Nic a new immune system, one that didn't carry the mutation. In his body, he would have two sets of DNA, one with and one without the mutation.

It worked! Years later, Nic is still alive. He can eat real food without triggering terrible and debilitating intestinal pain. He is not completely rehabilitated. The damage already done resulted in a seizure disorder. But he is alive. A one in three billion discovery saved his life.

It was discovery that wouldn't have happened without Watson, Crick, or the pioneering researchers at The Medical College of Wisconsin's Human and Molecular Genetics Center.

In recent years, many lives have been saved or improved because of our understanding of the DNA molecule. But Nicholas Volker was the first person whose life was directly saved because of DNA sequencing technology.

There will be many more.

Watson and Crick searched and discovered. Microbiologists with insatiable thirst for more information and knowledge sequenced the entire human genome. Nic's medical team wisely took a novel approach to a vexing problem. These great scientists and doctors passionately searched for new information and understanding to fuel progress and enrich life.

They zagged.

Nicholas Volker lived, and many more will follow.

CHAPTER 33

PAGE RANK

"All truth passes through three stages: First, it is ridiculed; Second, it is violently opposed; Third, it is accepted as self-evident."

– Arthur Schopenhauer

In the late 1990s, the internet was rapidly growing into a worldwide phenomenon, and its brightest stars were the search engines. Companies like yahoo.com, excite.com, lycos.com, go.com, and others commanded incredibly high stock market valuations as they provided a precious commodity – knowledge.

People who wanted to find information on the World Wide Web needed a search engine such as yahoo.com to guide the way. Similar to today, the person typed their request into the search engine and it returned a list of suggested websites.

At the time, virtually all of the search engines used the same methodology for cataloging and indexing the burgeoning list of websites on the internet. The system they employed relied on counting the number of times words appeared on a webpage and then recording that information. Then, when a person entered a search, the engine would rank websites based on the number of times the site contained the queried words.

All search engines operated the same way and returned the same results. This made them all easy to trick. Websites "stuffed" their pages with commonly searched words artificially inflating their ranking. And these search engines with simple, easy to manipulate algorithms produced mediocre results.

Against this backdrop in 1996, two young Ph. D candidates at Stanford University, Larry Page (age 24) and Sergey Brin (aged 23) embarked on a research project that would revolutionize internet search. Instead of taking the conventional approach to building search engines, they devised a novel way to solve the problem.

Their method employed an algorithm that ranked websites by counting the number and quality of other sites linking to its pages. Their model, known as PageRank, crawled through the World Wide Web and did more than count the number of words on a page.* It evaluated the number and quality of other websites that linked to a given site.

The breakthrough insight was that linking to another page required a deliberate choice by a webpage operator. The webmaster would have to view the other page and assess its worth before deciding to link to it. In essence, linking one's webpage to another was an explicit recommendation for the linked page. It was a conscious

---

* The name "PageRank" actually derives from Larry Page's last name, not from the algorithm that ranks web pages.

assessment of its value by someone who made the choice to tie their own property to it. This was something no algorithm or word counting search engine could accomplish. PageRank's methodological breakthrough enabled it to effectively measure website quality.

The following model provides a simplified, graphical representation of how PageRank evaluates websites. In the diagram, each circle depicts a website and each arrow represents a link. The percentage equals PageRank's calculation of the probability that a person randomly clicking on links would land on that webpage.* For example, in the diagram below, the probability that someone would land on page B equals 38.4%.

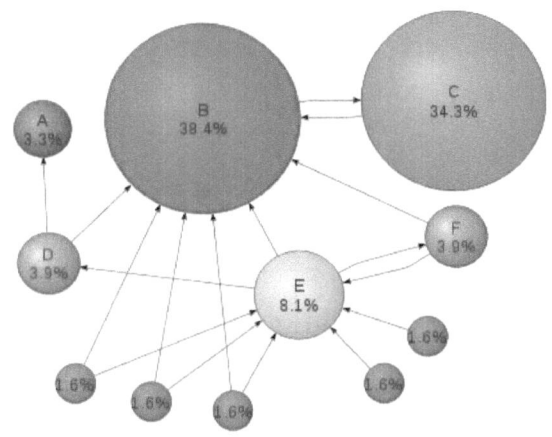

At first glance, the gap between Page C (34.3%) and Page E (8.1%) appears to be an error. Page C is ranked

---

* Page and Brin also employed other factors in their approach that have been excluded in the interest of brevity. Two factors are essential to the algorithm: 1) A "damping factor" that accounts for the fact that a web surfer would eventually stop clicking on links. 2) "Sink" adjustments to account for websites that have no links to other pages.

much higher despite having only one link while E has 6 inbound links. This apparent mistake actually highlights an aspect of PageRank that makes it successful. Page C ranks higher because its inbound link comes from the extremely popular Page B while E's links all come from relatively unpopular pages. If a very popular website chooses to link to another, that provides a much stronger endorsement than several links from obscure pages.

The new approach led to better search results.

Page and Brin named their search engine "Google." And it flourished.

In December 1998, *PC Magazine* named Google the search engine of choice in their annual Top 100 Websites List, proclaiming that it has "an uncanny knack for returning extremely relevant results." From there, the young company continued to grow and expand at a fantastic rate. After building a commanding lead and a powerful brand in search, Google leveraged its position to develop a lucrative advertising model and extend into several other profitable business segments.

In 2015, Page and Brin rolled Google and their other subsidiaries into a conglomerate called Alphabet Inc. At the time of this printing, Alphabet's stock market capitalization of approximately $560 billion makes it the 2nd most valuable company in the world. And, according to Forbes.com, Page and Brin were the 12th and 13th richest people in the world with an estimated net worth of about $35 billion each. What started as a novel approach to internet search blossomed into one of the world's largest and most successful companies.

Page and Brin chose to take a different path than all the other search engines of the day. When confronted with the same problem and the same information and access as their peers, they devised a unique way to use that information. Instead of blindly following their rivals, they thought differently and pioneered a better approach to internet search.

But Page and Brin didn't just create another engine. They shifted the way the entire industry thought about search. Today, nearly every search website uses algorithms with back-links as an input. Like other revolutions in science, eventually everyone will adopt the thinking and accept it as self-evident.

But, in the late 1990s, during the formative years of internet search, it was not self-evident. Page and Brin's unique approach enabled them to build a commanding and dominant lead. By the time others caught up, Google had built an incredible and sustainable business.

Today, Google is exploring several new technologies to leverage information. One of the more publicized endeavors is their self-driving car project. Google believes they can greatly improve the safety and efficiency of travel by developing cars that drive themselves.

The cars would leverage Google's vast database of information acquired through Google Maps and Google Earth for navigation. The cars would continually acquire new information from their surroundings like the location of nearby cars and the color of traffic lights. Google's technology would quickly process all this information enabling safe and efficient travel on the same roads alongside cars driven by people.

If Google is successful and Schopenhauer is right that "All truth passes through three stages: First, it is ridiculed; Second, it is violently opposed; Third, it is accepted as self-evident." Then:

<u>First</u>: Don't be surprised when you hear people scoff at the fantastical notion of self-driving cars.

<u>Second</u>: Don't be alarmed when regulators warn about the safety issues and violently oppose the idea.

<u>Third</u>: Don't be amazed when, several years from now, you and all of your neighbors have driverless cars parked in your garages.

CHAPTER 34

REVERSING THE CURSE

"I always admire people who have the courage to confront the conventional wisdom - I mean, people within the system. Those of us on the outside, it's easy for us to say whatever we think, because there are no consequences to it. It's much harder to say, 'I think the conventional wisdom is full of beans, and I'm not going to go along with it,' when you're inside the system and exposed to the possibility of actual failure. I think the people who do this drive the world to get better, whereas the people who snipe at anybody who dares suggest that the conventional wisdom is malarkey are, in my view, gutless conspirators in the mediocrity of the universe."

– Bill James

On December 26, 1919, in perhaps the worst deal in Major League Baseball history, the Boston Red Sox sold slugger Babe Ruth to their rival the New York Yankees. Prior to the deal, the Boston Red Sox experienced tremendous success having won World Series titles in 1903,

1912, 1915, 1916, and 1918.* The Yankees, on the other hand, prior to acquiring Ruth, never even participated in a World Series.

Babe Ruth, affectionately known as the "Bambino" and the "Sultan of Swat" had immediate, unprecedented, and unrivaled success with the Yankees. Over the course of his legendary career, Ruth set numerous records including establishing career bests for Home Runs (HR) and Runs Batted In (RBI). In 1920, his first year as a Yankee, Ruth blasted a staggering 54 Home Runs and achieved a remarkable 0.847 slugging percentage. Both set new league records.

Ruth's slugging record wouldn't be matched for 80 years, but his home run mark better evidences Ruth's domination of the game.† In 1920, only one team managed to hit more home runs than the Babe did all by himself.‡

For additional perspective, by the time Babe Ruth retired in 1935, he had hit 714 home runs. The next guy on the list was teammate Lou Gehrig who had just 353, and at that time, only ten other men had hit more than 200. Ruth simply dominated the game. Nearly 100 years later, he still holds numerous records, and during his time, his individual offensive output routinely dwarfed that of entire teams. Many still consider Ruth the greatest hitter in baseball history.

---

* The World Series is the championship for Major League Baseball. The first modern World Series was played in 1903. In the series, the Red Sox defeated the Pittsburgh Pirates claiming the championship.
† In 2001, Barry Bonds became the only player to ever have a higher single season slugging percentage (0.863) eclipsing Ruth's record.
‡ The Phillies hit 64 homeruns compared to Ruth's 54.

INFORMATION

In addition to his incredible individual achievements, Ruth elevated the play of his entire team. In 1921, just two years after Ruth's arrival, the Yankees won their first World Series. Ruth's acquisition had catapulted the once moribund franchise to the top of the league.

Ruth's early success helped the Yankees build a new stadium officially known as "Yankee Stadium." But it was appropriately nicknamed "The House that Ruth Built," for Ruth's tremendous box-office appeal enabled the Yankees to afford the large and modern facility.*

The momentum continued for the Yankees. Buoyed by Ruth's record-breaking performances, robust box-office receipts from their new stadium, and wise player acquisitions such as Lou Gehrig in the 1923 draft, the Yankees would win three more World Series titles during Ruth's career.

Even more importantly than capturing those first four World Series crowns, Ruth and the Yankees built a brand and a fiercely loyal fan base located in the vibrant New York marketplace. These factors combined to grant the Yankees a cumulative advantage that endures to this day.

---

* Yankee Stadium, opened in 1923, was the first "triple-deck" stadium in baseball history and seated 56,000 people, a staggering amount for the time. In the first game ever played at Yankee stadium, the Yankees defeated the Red Sox 4-1 behind the strength of a 3-run home run by Babe Ruth. The Yankees would win the World Series that season. Yankee Stadium would serve as the team's home until the 2008 season. On August 16, 2009, on the anniversary of Babe Ruth's death, the Yankees broke ground on another cutting-edge stadium "The New Yankee Stadium." As if scripted, the Yankees would win their record 27th World Series in the park's inaugural season.

Over the years, the Yankees have appeared in a record 40 World Series and won a record 27 Championships. This near-century of dominance all started with the acquisition of Babe Ruth from the Red Sox the day after Christmas in 1919. While Christmas came a day late for the Yankees in 1919, the gift they received proved to be timeless.

The Yankee's gift was the Red Sox' curse. The sale of Ruth marked a dramatic change in trajectory for both franchises. In stark contrast to the Yankees, the Red Sox, once frequent champions, took a sudden dive as a franchise. Following the sale of Ruth, the Red Sox endured an 86-year drought where they would fail to win another World Series. This drought would become known as the "Curse of the Bambino."

Not only did the Red Sox fail to win, they frequently lost in heartbreaking fashion. In 1946, the Red Sox made their first trip to the World Series since trading Ruth only to lose the final game on a highly unusual play. In the play, now known by baseball historians as the "Mad Dash," St. Louis Cardinal and Hall of Fame inductee, Enos "Country" Slaughter scrambled home all the way from first base after ignoring his coach's signal to stop. Slaughter scored the decisive run costing the Red Sox the World Series.

Decades later, in 1978, still mired in the middle of their World Series drought, the Red Sox held a commanding lead in the standings late in the season. They appeared to be the team to beat and talk of the World Series permeated discussions among the Red Sox faithful. Yet, and almost predictably, the Red Sox blew their large lead to the hated Yankees.

The two rivals ended the regular season deadlocked in the standings forcing a 1-game playoff. In the playoff, the Red Sox held a 2-0 lead until an unlikely hero emerged for the Yankees. Bucky Dent, known now in pubs around Boston as "Bucky-F'ing-Dent," a player not known for his power, blasted a 3-run homer to give the Yankees a 3-2 lead. The Yankees would win the World Series that year, and the Red Sox would mourn another excruciating loss.

Later in 1986, the Red Sox appeared poised to break the curse. They took a 3-2 game lead into Game 6 of the 1986 World Series versus the New York Mets. In the final inning, the Red Sox led 5-3 with two outs. They were just one out away from capturing the elusive title when the unthinkable happened. The Mets' Mookie Wilson dribbled a routine ground ball up the first base line directly toward veteran Red Sox first baseman Bill Buckner. It should have been a routine play, an easy out. Buckner had made a similar play successfully literally thousands of times in his career. Not this time. The ball went right through his legs allowing the Mets to win the game. The Mets then won the decisive game 7. The Red Sox consistently snatched defeat from the jaws of victory. The Curse continued.

Sabermetrics

To evaluate players, teams utilize both objective statistical comparisons and subjective evaluations of experts to inform their personnel decisions. Historically, statistical evaluation focused on a few benchmark statistics such as batting average, Runs Batted In, and Home Runs.

These measures have been tracked over time and are easily computed for all players. These core statistics also have tremendous appeal with baseball fans. These simple statistics allow enthusiasts to compare batting averages, RBI, and HR totals for the game's all-time greats such as Ruth and Gehrig with modern day players like Barry Bonds and Alex Rodriguez.

In addition to objective statistical analysis, teams evaluate current players and future prospects based on the subjective evaluations of experts. To find young talent, teams enlist an army of scouts and deploy them throughout the world in a quest to find new players. They frequent college and high school baseball games and they travel to sandlots in developing parts of the world in search of talent. The subjective assessment of these scouts helps inform a team's decision to acquire a player during the league's annual amateur draft.

To evaluate experienced talent already on professional team rosters, teams also rely heavily on subjective assessment. In this case, scouts still play an important role, but the assessment of the team's executives and owners is usually decisive.

Unlike with young talent playing on a remote sandlot in another country, experienced talent plays in more assessable and visible locations to General Managers and team owners. Naturally, General Managers and owners tend to form their own opinion about certain players and use their assessments to inform their player acquisition strategy.

As the story of Babe Ruth illustrates, the decision to acquire or trade a player can determine a team's fortunes for a very long time and in a very significant way. Of course, not all decisions have the enduring impact of the infamous sale of Babe Ruth But, nonetheless, decisions about a team's roster will determine the team's success from season to season.

Baseball is a game blessed with a robust history, a charming lore, and a penchant for statistics. It is also a game riddled with unwritten rules, conventional wisdom, and a reliance on subjective assessment. It is a game where the trade of a single player can mean so much to the future of a team. It is also a game, where for over a century, nearly every single team used essentially the same set of statistics and method of subjective player assessment. These same methods formed the backbone of every team's player evaluation strategies and ultimately determined who teams drafted, traded, and acquired.

It was an approach embraced by virtually all – until Bill James came along.

Bill James was an obsessive baseball fan and writer who chose to think differently than his contemporaries. For evaluating talent, the conventional approach involved comparing a player's performance against established statistics. For batters, teams focused on statistics such as Batting Average, RBIs, and Home Runs. For pitchers, they focused on Win-Loss record and Earned Run Average (ERA).

James took a different approach. He reasoned that a player's contribution to his team depended on his ability to help the team win games. To help a team win, a batter needed to create more runs for his team and a pitcher needed to help keep the other team from scoring.

He reasoned that the traditional statistics didn't do a great job of teasing out the contributions of an individual player. For example, a player's RBI total is strongly dependent on the ability of other players on his team to get on base and into scoring position before the player even gets to bat. With the Win-Loss record for pitchers, a pitcher's record strongly depends on his team's ability to score runs while the pitcher is just sitting on the bench. Both of these traditional statistics are severely limited in that they are heavily influenced by factors completely out of the player's control.

James found traditional statistics lacking in that they often posed vexing questions without a clear answer. For example, would a team be better off with a player who had a very high batting average, but hit only a few home runs, or with a player with a low batting average but who hit a lot of home runs? These types of questions served as barroom fodder for centuries among baseball aficionados with the cognoscente having mixed opinions.

James solved both of these fundamental issues by creating a range of statistics that focused on a player's individual contributions and linked them to a common denominator – runs scored.

For hitters, he created a new statistic to evaluate players, "Runs Created." This statistic attempts to quantify the number of runs a player creates for his team. For pitchers, he eschewed traditional Win-Loss and ERA in favor of a new statistic he named "Game Score" which calculated the performance of a pitcher in any given game focusing on those aspects more in the pitcher's control.

James created numerous new measures to evaluate a player's individual contributions linking many of them to the common denominator of runs.* For the most part, James's new statistics were simple to understand, easy to calculate, and more effective than traditional approaches. The movement to use advanced statists to objectively measure baseball performance would become known as Sabermetrics, a name coined by James.†

James created an abundance of new statistics, many of which James and subsequent generations of Sabermetricians would continue to improve upon. However, James's contribution extended far beyond creating a few new statistics. While his statistics were important, his underlying ideas were more enduring and revolutionary.

In addition to focusing on an individual's contributions to a team's ability to win, James championed other non-conventional perspectives. With regard to fielding ability, James argued that the traditional "Fielding Percentage"

---

* Later, James and other Sabermetricians would extend the common denominator of "runs" into "wins" using relatively simple calculations. Further extrapolation and comparison to an average or "replacement" player led to even more advanced and practical statistics such as WARP (Wins Above Replacement Player) which allowed comparison of a player's contribution to wins versus a theoretical average player. Players across the league and across positions could then be compared to each other based on the thing that mattered most, their ability to help their team win games relative to a player that they could be replaced by in the lineup.

† Sabermetrics is a derivative of the acronym (SABR) an abbreviation for the Society for American Baseball Research.

metric, which calculates the percent of defensive fielding opportunities successfully handled, fails in that it doesn't account for a great defender's ability to get to certain balls and make more plays. In James's view, the more outs a defender participates in is a much better gauge of his defensive ability.

He also championed the notion of a "defensive spectrum." He reasoned that some defensive positions are more difficult to play, and therefore, more difficult and important to fill on a roster. Accordingly, he placed a premium on players that play more difficult positions, and argued that those who play easier defensive positions would have to compensate with even stronger offensive performance.

He also contributed new thinking in the area of drafting pitchers. In the annual amateur draft, teams take turns selecting from an available pool of players for their teams. Many of the available players currently play in college while many are still in high school. When it came to drafting pitchers, James had a novel theory that he studied thoroughly. Based on his research, James argued that teams would be better off drafting pitchers in college with their top picks than drafting players in high school. At the time, conventional thinking, largely shaped by the opinion of subjective talent scout evaluations, held that younger high school players had more "upside" and therefore were more valuable.

Like with many great insights, in hindsight, they often seem obvious. But at the time, much of James' thinking wasn't obvious. In fact, many of the concepts he developed in the late 1970s and mid-1980s would not be widely utilized for decades.

One of the first teams to commit to running a baseball team based on Sabermetrics was the Oakland A's in the late 1990s. Oakland had a small payroll relative to the other teams in the league. In 2002, the A's paid their entire team just over $40 million dollars ranking them 28th in the 30-team league in spending. In contrast, the team with the largest payroll, the Yankees ($126M) outspent the A's by a factor of more than 3 to 1. On a per player basis, the Yankees paid an average player $4.3 million and the A's just $1.48 million.*

Because they had a relatively small payroll, the A's needed to devise a non-traditional approach to compete. The team's management reasoned that they needed to identify and acquire players that the rest of the league undervalued. To select these players, they turned to Sabermetrics.

Starting in the late 1990s, the A's General Manager Billy Beane began assembling a roster using the new approach.† In 1999, the Oakland A's would post their first winning record in 7 years. In 2000, they would make it to the playoffs for the first time in nearly a decade. After return trips to the playoffs in 2001 and 2002, the entire league marveled at the miraculous turnaround in Oakland.

---

* Yes, I understand that I wrote "just" $1.48 million dollars. While it seems a bit ludicrous, one must keep in mind that relatively speaking it was less than 1/3 of what the Yankees paid their average player.
† Beane was later portrayed by Brad Pitt in the 2011 film *Moneyball*. The film chronicles the story of Beane and the Oakland A's and the success they achieved by employing Sabermetrics.

The recently moribund franchise with the puny payroll had become a playoff regular. Sabermetrics had crossed the chasm from theoretical discussion among baseball statisticians to practical and successful application in Major League Baseball.

The Reverse

In February 2002, John Henry bought the Boston Red Sox. Henry made his fortune in the financial markets by making dispassionate and objective investments on commodities like soybeans, foreign currency, and interest rates. Henry's approach relied upon removing all traces of human emotion and any subjective judgment whatsoever from his decisions. To accomplish this, he built advanced statistical models to identify investments that the rest of the market undervalued and overvalued. When he found an investment that was overvalued, he sold. When he found one that was undervalued, he bought. A baseball fan his entire life with an astute analytical and objective mind, he found Sabermetrics extremely compelling and decided to employ its principles with the Red Sox.

Henry grew up reading Bill James's books and articles, and when he became owner of the Red Sox, he quickly hired two people to lead the implementation of a Sabermetrics informed personnel strategy. First, after a failed approach to lure Oakland A's manager Billy Beane, he hired some bright young up and comer, Theo Epstein. Second, he hired Bill James in an advisory capacity. Upon the hiring of James, Epstein commented: "What Bill offers us, more than a particular set of sophisticated statistical formulas, is a way of thinking. Bill doesn't start with an assumption and then find data to support it, like a lot of people in baseball do. Bill starts with a question, and then he does the research objectively and doggedly, and lets the truth empirically come to him."

To the Red Sox, James brought a new way of thinking. And the Red Sox had one major advantage that the A's lacked. Unlike the low-budget A's, the Red Sox personnel budget trailed only the Yankees. Sabermetrics added brains to the Red Sox' financial brawn.

Prior to Henry purchasing the team, the Red Sox labored in an eight-decade long World Series drought. They had finished second in their division the last three years, each year trailing their arch rival New York Yankees. Then, starting in late 2002, reformed by James and fully embracing a new approach, the Red Sox made a large number of personnel moves. In January and February 2003, they acquired Bill Mueller, David Ortiz, and Kevin Millar. Following the 2003 season, in November and December they acquired pitcher Curt Schilling and second baseman Mark Bellhorn. During the 2004 season, at the trade deadline, they acquired outfielder Dave Roberts.

In the 2003 season, the Red Sox returned to the playoffs only to lose to the Yankees. In 2004, the Red Sox made the playoffs once again and appeared on the verge of losing to their nemesis yet again. The Red Sox lost the first three games in a seven-game series with the Yankees. One more loss and the Red Sox would have failed again.

To win the series, they needed to stage a miraculous and unprecedented comeback. Amazingly, they did, and the players most responsible for the turnaround were the ones acquired after the Red Sox employed Sabermetrics.

In game 4, in their final at bat, the Red Sox trailed 4-3. And that's when the curse started to reverse...

Kevin Millar (2003 acquisition) walked, pinch runner Dave Roberts (2004) stole second base, and Bill Mueller (2003) singled, scoring Roberts and tying the game. Later in the 12th inning, David Ortiz (2003) blasted a 2-run home run to win the game. From the jaws of defeat, the Red Sox had snared victory.

Game 5 also went to extra innings, and the Red Sox prevailed behind the strength of another Ortiz HR and his game winning single in the 14th inning. Game 6 resulted in yet another dramatic Red Sox victory. Curt Shilling (2003) pitched a heroic game on an injured ankle and visibly bloody sock and Mark Bellhorn (2003) added a 3-run home run.

The Red Sox would dominate Game 7, vanquish the rival Yankees, and return to the World Series. In so doing, the Red Sox became the first team in history to come back from a 0-3 series disadvantage and win a 7-game series.

In the World Series, the Red Sox handily defeated the St. Louis Cardinals, sweeping the 7-game series 4-0. Eighty-six years after the Red Sox sold Babe Ruth to the Yankees, the Red Sox were World Champions again.

The curse had been reversed.*

---

* When he was hired, Epstein became the youngest GM in MLB history at just 28 years of age. After this time with the Red Sox,

CHAPTER 35

A CAUTIONARY TALE

"The maxim 'Nothing but perfection' may be spelled 'Paralysis'."

– Winston Churchill

Originally written down in ancient Greece between 620 and 560 BC by a story-telling slave, the collection of parables now known as *Aesop's Fables* contains a number of tales, each containing a moral lesson.

One allegory contained in Aesop's cannon is the story of the Fox and the Cat. In the anecdote, the cunning fox boasts to the cat that he has hundreds of ways of evading hunters. To his dismay, the cat confesses that he has only one method of escape. When the fox and cat hear the hunter's, hounds approaching in the distance, the cat

---

Epstein would become the General Manager of the Chicago Cubs. When he took over, the Cubs were one of the worst teams in baseball. Five years later, in 2016, after completely rebuilding the team using Sabermetrics principles, the Cubs would win their first World Series championship since 1908. Another all-time curse, the curse of the Billy Goat, had been reversed.

quickly scampers up a tree to safety, while the fox remains in place on the ground busy contemplating which of his many methods of escape he should employ.

The cunning and strategic fox is trapped by the hounds while the decisive cat successfully eludes the hunters. The fable ends with the lesson: "Better one safe way than a hundred on which you cannot reckon."

The parable teaches that having more options is not always better. It is often better to be quick and decisive than cunning and slow. Likewise, gathering more and more information doesn't always ensure better decisions. When confronted by too many options and too much information, people are often paralyzed by the sheer complexity and scope of the decision. Other times, people, like the Fox, become incapacitated by their quest for the perfect solution to a problem. Caught up in analysis, they fail to act.

Malcolm Gladwell astutely noted in Blink, "We live in a world that assumes that the quality of a decision is directly related to the time and effort that went into making it...We believe that we are always better off gathering as much information as possible and spending as much time as possible in deliberation." People have a bias to gather more information than necessary to make a decision, subscribing to the false and nearly pervasive belief that more information is better.

In the medical field, this irrational quest for additional information is commonplace, and it contributes to excessive medical testing and skyrocketing medical costs. Some suggest the overabundance of medical testing stems from disingenuous profit motives or the fear of frivolous lawsuits. While these may be contributing factors, part of the blame should be placed on the pervasive belief that more information is better.

The logic of the test-happy medical community appears to be sound at first blush. The thinking goes: "Of course we should get more information; a patient's health is at stake. This is a matter of life and death. The more information we have available to make a decision will give us a better opportunity to save the patient's life." While this seems reasonable, new information often doesn't alter the course of treatment. While some information may be "nice to know," if it doesn't change the treatment, it isn't valuable.

Imagine you are a doctor and your patient has symptoms that suggest that he has disease A with 80% probability, disease B with 10% probability, and disease C with 10% probability. Each disease is completely curable, but each disease requires a completely different treatment.

If presented with a diagnostic test that would signal positive if the patient had disease B, negative if the patient had disease C, and indicate positive or negative with equal likelihood if the patient had disease A. Would you conduct the test?

In this fictitious example, many people will recommend conducting the test. More information is better of course. This is a matter of life and death. But a closer examination of the impact on decision making confirms that the test has no real value.

After administering the test to all 100 people, one would find that half the people tested positive and half the people tested negative. Those who tested positive would have Disease A 80% of the time (40/50) and Disease B 20% of the time (10/50). Those who tested negative would have Disease A 80% of the time (40/50) and Disease C 20% of the time (10/50). After the test, 80% of people who test positive or negative will have Disease A – just like before the test was administered.*

The doctor will prescribe the same treatment regardless of the test result. Because of the prevalence of Disease A and the lack of clarity gained from testing, the doctor would end up treating the patient for Disease A either way. The test was absolutely useless because it didn't change the course of action.

The lesson learned from this contrived hypothetical example holds true in the real world. More testing may create more information, but not necessarily more

---

* The following table details the probabilities associated with this hypothetical example assuming there are 100 people presenting with symptoms.

	Disease A	Disease B	Disease C	Total
People out of 100 with the disease	80	10	10	100
Number that would test positive	40	10	0	50
Number that would test negative	40	0	10	50

knowledge. The end result of administering another expensive test is often a higher medical bill and inoculation against a lawsuit, but not a change in the course of treatment. Many smart medical practitioners understand this, and as a result, treat for common illnesses before testing for rare maladies. If an otherwise healthy patient presents with a cough, smart doctors treat for chest congestion from the common cold before they administer an MRI.

But in the real world, things aren't always as straightforward as in these simple examples. Multiple factors cloud the issue. The odds of having a particular disease aren't clearly laid out in a grid, and the health of real people hangs in the balance. Even in sterile experimental conditions, people tend to overvalue additional information. In the real world, when the issues and tradeoffs are even murkier, the tendency to covet additional information intensifies. As a result, people seek more and more information even when it cannot affect action.

This bias isn't relegated to the medical field. Companies will conduct excessive and unnecessary market research studies delaying the launches of new products. Sometimes the additional research improves the offering, but often it just delays the launch. Governments form commissions to endlessly study and evaluate new ideas while progress is delayed. People vacillate before making purchases, researching and testing, but not learning anything that will change their eventual purchase decision.

The drive to acquire more information and to conduct more analysis leads to paralysis which often leads to last minute blunders. In sports, it's called "choking." An athlete thinks too much about a particular play, locks up, and then in the last moment hastily makes a mistake. In chess, it is called Kotov Syndrome. The player faces a complicated decision, analyzes every option over and over again, and then with time running low, makes a quick and ill-advised move.

Today, the issue is compounded by the incredible amount of data available in the world. Information is cheap and readily accessible, often with the simple click of a mouse.

When dealing with a complicated issue, mountains of information, and limited time, Albert Einstein recommends spending sufficient time correctly defining the problem. If only given an hour, perhaps the greatest mind of the last century, said he would spend 55 minutes thinking about the problem and a mere 5 minutes on the solution. For Einstein, a properly framed problem statement is the key to an effective and elegant solution.

An apocryphal allegory from the apex of the space race between the US and the Russians highlights the importance of a properly framed question. As the story goes, during the space race, the Americans spent millions of dollars in a quest to develop a pen capable of writing in zero gravity. It took the United States countless hours and a lot of money to develop the pen. To achieve the same end objective of zero gravity writing, the Russians spent just a few minutes and less than a ruble. The Russians just used a pencil.

INFORMATION

The Americans framed the problem incorrectly: develop a pen to write in zero gravity.

The Russians framed the problem in a way that enabled the elegant solution: Write in zero gravity.

Post Script

People can thrive in a world of imperfect information. Humans are endowed with an amazing ability to process limited slices of information effectively and to quickly and effortlessly organize disparate pieces of data into unified wholes. But since information is rarely perfect or complete, people suffer from the same biases and succumb to the same types of mistakes.

Many have conquered these challenges, and leveraged information to zag. Some have used information to their advantage on the battlefield. Others have achieved greatness through discovering new information that improves life for all. Some have chosen to process information in a novel way that produces superior results.

But there is a cautionary tale to keep in mind. Contrary to conventional thinking, more information is not always better, and more time spent contemplating a decision doesn't always yield a better answer. Beware of the biases. Answer the right question. And act decisively like the cat to avoid being paralyzed by options, crushed under a mountain of data, and bound to the shoal.

Part Six

Conformity

CHAPTER 36

NO SOAP RADIO!

"Two penguins are sitting in a bathtub. The first one says, "Can you please pass the soap?" The second one says, "No soap radio!"

– Version of a traditional anti-humor joke popular in the 1950s and 1960s.

"No soap radio!" is a punch line used in a prank popular in the United States in the 1950s and 1960s. While many versions of the joke exist, the basic set-up and punch line are similar. In the ruse, the joke teller and a couple confederates aim to trick an unwitting victim.

To begin the deception, the trickster announces that he or she is about to tell a funny joke. After the victim and the confederates have gathered to listen, the jokester delivers a set-up that usually involves some combination of animals in a bathtub such as: "Two penguins are sitting in a bathtub. The first one says, 'Can you please pass the soap?'" Next, the joke teller delivers the punch line: "The second one says, 'No soap radio!'" Upon hearing the nonsensical and unrelated punch line, the prankster and his or her accomplices start to laugh uproariously.

261

The joke doesn't make any sense, but the joke teller and his or her coconspirators have placed their intended victim in a difficult position. On one hand, the victim could remain silent revealing their confusion. But doing so would risk embarrassment in front of the group for failing to understand the obviously hilarious joke. On the other hand, the victim could join in the laughter and pretend that the joke is actually funny, conforming to the behavior of the group.

To conform, or not to conform? That is the predicament.

Undoubtedly, on the playgrounds across the United States, numerous children fell victim to the "No Soap Radio!" joke by conforming and laughing to the great pleasure of the joker teller and their conspirators. But how frequently would people actually feign laughter at a nonsensical joke? Or, perhaps more importantly, how frequently would adults actually pretend to agree with something that they knew was obviously incorrect? Would people conform to the beliefs of a group even if they knew them to be wrong?

Solomon Asch, an American pioneer in the field of social psychology, designed a now famous experiment to answer these types of questions. In his Conformity Experiments, Asch recruited participants for what they believed to be a series of vision tests. The participants were placed into groups along with accomplices of the experimenter. Just like in the "No Soap Radio!" jokes, the coconspirators knew the true objectives of the experiment. And the test administrator, just like the joke teller, set up the test to put the unknowing participant in a tough predicament.

In the test, the administrator shows the participant and several confederates a line printed on a card. Next, the administrator shows a card with lines labeled A, B, and C. The participants were then asked to identify the line on the second card that matched the length of the first line.

An example of the lines that were used is pictured below.

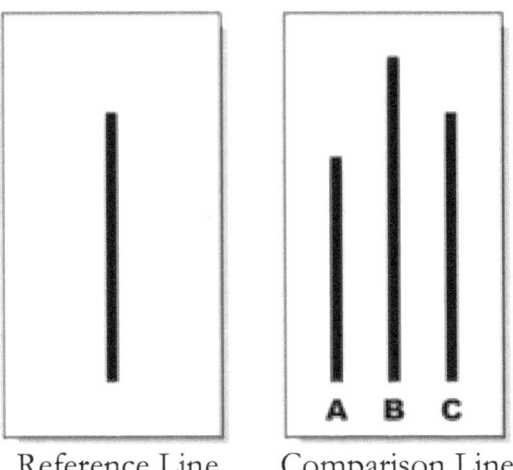

Reference Line   Comparison Lines

So, which line on the second card matches the length of the first reference line?

The answer is pretty obvious, right? It is "B."

Just kidding.

The answer is indeed "C." But ask yourself – did the suggestion of "B" give you pause? Perhaps not, but what if several other people in the same room verbalized the answer "B" first? Would you conform and say "B" even though the answer is clearly "C"?

At the start of his study, Solomon Asch didn't think that people would conform to a belief that was so obviously wrong. But his famous experiment proved otherwise. In his landmark test, 75% of all participants would conform at least once, with an astoundingly high 37% conformity rate over all of the trials. In other words, 37% of the time people stated the wrong answer just because everyone else did.

Asch's experiment also included a control group consisting of 35 people. In the control group, the participants were shown the same exact stimuli as those in the test group. In the control group, in 18 trials across 35 participants for a total of 630 trials, only one of the participants ever gave an incorrect answer. These weren't tough questions at all. The participants in the test group knew the right answers, but under pressure to conform, they knowingly gave the wrong answers.

Similar to the other factors that lead to conventional thinking and behavior, the pressure to conform is a powerful force. And this phenomenon isn't relegated to just trivial situations such as identifying the length of a line or choosing to laugh at a nonsensical joke. When making important decisions, the primal need to conform drives people to join the shoal. To zag, one must overcome this powerful desire to think and act differently.

CHAPTER 37

MADNESS & HYSTERIA

"I can calculate the motion of heavenly bodies, but not the madness of people."

– Sir Isaac Newton

Social psychologists who study crowd psychology offer differing explanations for how a crowd can take on a life of its own. Some suggest that there is an evolutionary reason why people depersonalize and conform to the group. They reason that following the group enabled the ancestors of modern humans to more effectively hunt, practice agriculture, and migrate to more hospitable environments.

Others argue that humans are born with a common collective unconsciousness that leads all people to organize and experience things similarly. These shared archetypes lead to similar reactions to the same environment resulting in an instinctually created crowd experience.

Some believe that like-minded crowds are the product of a natural convergence of like-minded individuals. With this theory, the crowd doesn't create common behavior, it is merely an aggregation of people who thought and behaved similarly in the first place.

These theories all have merit and each offer a different lens with which to view and analyze crowd behavior. And, practically speaking, not all crowds are created the same. Some are small and some are large. Some are benign while others are destructive.

Regardless if a crowd's behavior is governed by evolutionary, instinctual, or convergence reasons, the group's will often supersede that of the individuals that constitute the collective. In these cases, individuals act like animals, just like a shoal of sardines, a herd of cattle, or a throng of lemmings. Influenced by their membership in the crowd, people conform and act, not of their own accord or volition, but as a mindless drone.

Madness

Just a few decades after the Ottomans introduced the tulip to Europe, the flower became a highly-coveted luxury item. The Dutch, in particular, grew particularly enamored with the bulbous plant. In the Netherlands, enterprising tulip growers experimented with various horticultural techniques to create new and stunning varietals. The tulip proprietors of the day, excellent marketers as they were, created spectacular and regal sounding brand names for their tulip varieties such as "The Viceroy" or "Admiral of Admirals." Buoyed by horticultural advances, clever marketing, and the growing wealth of the region, the popularity of the tulip continued to grow strongly into the early 1600s.

The protracted lifecycle of the spring blooming perennial contributed to the eventual mania surrounding its bulbs. Tulips sprout from bulbs that bloom in the early spring. After the initial bloom in April or May, tulip growers could uproot and transport the bulbs between June and September. During this short four-month span, a market existed for the flowers where a customer could purchase a flowering bulb from a proprietor and replant it in their own garden. For this third of the year, the market for tulips was similar to most markets. A seller offered a complete product to a buyer for an immediate sale. Between June and September, buying a tulip was just like going down to the local grocery store to purchase a jug of milk.

But, during the remainder of the year, no blooming tulips were available for sale. A person couldn't observe the flower of the plant – only the bulb. Adding to the complexity of the situation, the best and most coveted varietals would take as long as 7-12 years to cultivate.

These complications did not deter the inventive Dutch. In response to the growing market demand and the unique lifecycle of the tulip, the Dutch created futures contracts for the highly-prized bulbs. In the contracts, people would agree to purchase tulips at a later date at a predetermined price. No longer were tulip sales confined to the months of June through September.

With the invention of the contracts, people could buy tulips all year round. More interestingly, people could now begin to speculate on future prices. No longer were tulips just a beautiful flower. Now, they were a prized commodity that could be easily traded and speculated on all year round, just like a share of a company's stock.

The more people who bought, the higher their prices became, and as a result, the more attractive they became as status symbols. As prices continued to rise, more and more Dutch clambered for the bulbs as symbols of their success.

What started out as a peculiar fascination with a beautiful flower would spiral into a full-blown mania. The futures markets opened up tulip speculation to people who never cared to own a tulip themselves, but rather, who desired to profit from trading in the rapidly rising market.

French investors joined the Dutch in the frenzy, and with added speculation, prices continued to skyrocket. Throngs of people, some who loved the flowers, others who loved the status they provided, and many who just wanted to profit on the trade all jumped headlong into the market.

The vicious vortex of speculation strengthened – buying begat more buying which begat even more buying – building an untenable bubble that would eventually burst. People formed a herd that fanatically bought tulip bulbs driving the market price up upward in a self-fulfilling manner. The more who bought, the higher the prices grew. The higher the prices, the more who joined in the mania. The more who joined, the more tulips were purchased driving the prices even higher. People didn't stop to think about the intrinsic value of the actual tulip they were purchasing, they just joined in the madness of the crowd.

In 1637, at the height of the hysteria and just before the inevitable crash, certain varieties of tulips were reportedly the most expensive items in the world. A single bulb of the variety branded "The Viceroy" sold for between 3,000-4,200 florins, roughly 10-14 times what a skilled craftsman of the time could earn annually.

In his classic book, *Extraordinary Popular Delusions and the Madness of Crowds*, Charles Mackay offers a colorful and amusing account of the Dutch tulip bulb mania. He chronicles other amazing examples of the extraordinary prices people were willing to pay for tulip bulbs. Someone exchanged 12 acres of land for a prized Semper Augustus bulb. Another purchased 40 bulbs for an astounding 100,000 florins. For perspective, those 100,000 florins could have purchased 3,333 fat swine or 1,000 tons of butter, or they could have paid the annual wages for 300 skilled craftsmen or 600 laborers. All for 40 tulips bulbs.

Eventually, in 1637, the bubble predictably burst. Tulip bulb prices plummeted.

Numerous speculative asset bubbles have propagated over the years and across cultures. Sometimes the bubble occurs in a real asset market such as the Japanese real estate bubble which burst in the early 1990s and the United States housing bubble which started to deflate in late-2006. Other times the bubble strikes in the stock market as it did with the "dot com" bubble which popped in 2000 and the roaring 20s bubble which popped just prior to the Great Depression.

Bubbles have developed in commodities markets such as the Uranium Bubble of 2007 and the Rhodium bubble of 2008. Sometimes bubbles remain isolated to a specific industry such as the Poseidon bubble that affected the Australian mining industry following the discovery of a promising source of nickel metal in 1969 and Railway mania which struck in Great Britain in the 1840s.

Countless speculative bubbles have cropped up overtime and across industries and cultures. With speculative bubbles, people tend to jettison reason and individuality and join the mad herd. Mackay famously wrote, "Men it has been well said, think in herds; it will be seen that they go mad in herds, while they only recover their senses slowly, and one by one."

Countless fortunes have been lost over the centuries by conforming and joining a mad herd of investors or speculators. When the bubble inevitably bursts, those left holding the devalued assets suffer tremendous losses.

But, while many conform, zig, and lose, a select few profit from boldly going in the opposite direction of the teeming masses. Baron Rothschild, who amassed a great fortune by aggressively buying while everyone else was selling following the Battle of Waterloo, offered this timeless advice: "Buy when there's blood in the streets, even if the blood is your own."

In other words, when everyone else zigs – zag.

Hysteria

When people conform, and join a mad herd in an asset bubble, they suffer significant financial loss. While unfortunate, these misfortunes pale in comparison to the tragedy that can ensue when the herd turns into an hysterical mob.

Often, when like-minded individuals assemble for a particular cause, their behavior can turn violent. The convergence into a group often destroys individual reasoning and suppresses inhibitions leading to violence and rioting. During these riots, individuals who wouldn't ever raise a fist in anger if alone, commit unspeakable acts of violence as their membership in the collective quashes their individuality.

Social causes often create the crucible for these hysterical mobs. This happened during the Los Angeles riots of 1992 following the acquittal of four Los Angeles police officers charged with beating a black man named Rodney King. Ironically, in a protest against unnecessary violence, 53 people died and rioters destroyed over $1 billion worth of property.

The 1863 New York City draft riots, the largest civil insurrection in United States history other than the Civil War, led to 120 deaths and left 2,000 people injured. The rioters, mostly working class men, began a peaceful protest about a new law passed by Congress that would make those unable to pay a $300 fee subject to conscription to the Union Army. The mad crowd quickly devolved into a race riot. Just like 1992 tragedy in Los Angeles, the New York riots started with people protesting the unfairness of government action on an underrepresented group and against violence. Also, like the LA riots, the hysterical mob spiraled out of control and ended in hate and catastrophic loss.

With both riots, like-minded people gathered to protest a perceived wrong. But once part of the collective, peaceful people grew violent and destructive. Some even murdered.

Sporting events also bring together many like-minded individuals, who once together, sometimes commit unspeakable acts as a group that they wouldn't consider perpetrating if they were alone. Fights often break out between opposing fans and hysterical mobs occasionally lead to trampling injuries or even death.

In 1985 in Brussels, during the notorious Heysel Stadium disaster, 39 fans were crushed to death. The match pitted the Italian team Juventus against the English team Liverpool in the Eastern Cup Final. About an hour before kickoff, rabid Liverpool fans breached a security fence and charged at the Juventus fans. In an attempt to flee to safety, the Juventus fans ran backwards into a concrete wall. Some escaped, but many didn't. They senselessly perished less than an hour before their favorite team competed for the championship.

Remarkably, the teams still played the game, even after the tragedy. The crowd was so hysterical that officials feared even more violence if they postponed the game. Juventus won the match 1-0, a small consolation prize to the families of the 39 who died. Normal people joined a crowd, became a mob, and committed unspeakable violence.

Sadly, the Heysel Stadium disaster is only one of many tragedies stemming from hysterical crowds with a mob mentality. That disaster wasn't even the largest loss of life involving Liverpool. Just a few years later in 1989, in what is known as the Hillsborough disaster, 96 Liverpool fans were crushed to death as they rushed to enter the arena and police were unable to safely corral the masses.

And modern day football (or soccer) riots don't even compare to the largest sports related riot of all time. In AD 532 in Constantinople, a large crowd gathered for chariot races at the Hippodrome which sat adjacent to Emperor Justinian's palace. From the confines of his complex, Justinian could comfortably observe the races.

Four teams competed in the races: the Blues, the Greens, the Reds, and the Whites. Emperor Justinian favored the Blues. Not surprisingly, the majority of the crowd also cheered for the Blues, effectively the home team supported by the Emperor.

Yet, not all was well in the Empire. Taxes were high. The Persians threatened the empire from the East. Over the course of the day, the crowd migrated from supporting the Blues, to cheering against the Blues, to eventually charging the castle and attempting to overthrow Emperor Justinian. In the end, half the city was destroyed and an estimated 30,000 people killed.

In each of these cases, individuals joined a crowd and then something terrible happened. The psychology of the crowd takes its members down a different path than the individuals in the crowd would go down alone. The hysterical mob robs its members of their individuality and inhibitions. It subjugates the individual's Superego-like freewill to the Id-like cravings of the collective.

CHAPTER 38

THE SELFISH HERD

"If all your friends jumped off the Brooklyn Bridge, would you jump off too?"

— My Mom

Biologists believe that some animal herding behavior is the product of uncoordinated and selfish actions of individual animals. When a predator approaches, each animal, in an attempt to avoid being killed, moves quickly to the safest spot possible. That spot is the center of the herd and furthest away from the approaching predators. This collection of individuals, each acting in their own best interests, appears like a coordinated herd of animals fleeing in unison. In reality, according to the proponents of this Selfish Herd theory, the observed herding behavior is not coordinated, but rather a collection of individuals trying to save themselves.

Imagine the shoal of sardines. When the dolphins approached, individual sardines moved closer and closer together into a tight bait ball. Unfortunately for the sardines, the tight grouping made each sardine an easier target for the eclectic collection of sea predators. Likewise, herding behavior in humans can occur without planning and when under attack. And, just like the sardines, the outcome is usually not a good one.

The Rise of General Motors

Founded in 1908, General Motors quickly grew to become one of the largest companies in the world. The company flourished under the leadership of one of the most successful American businessmen, Alfred P. Sloan, who served as the company's CEO and Chairman for decades.

General Motors surpassed Ford Motor Company in the late 1920s as the United States' leading automaker and continued to expand and strengthen its position through the 1950s. At its peak, General Motors had higher sales and more employees than any US company. They commanded a dominant market share, accounting for roughly half of US vehicles sales.

In 1953, President Eisenhower appointed the President of General Motors, Charles Erwin Wilson, as the new United States Secretary of Defense. During confirmation hearings, the Senate Armed Services Committee asked Wilson if he could set aside past allegiances and make decisions in the best interest of the nation but detrimental to GM.

After careful consideration, Wilson replied that he couldn't think of a situation when the interests of GM and the US wouldn't be aligned, "because for years I thought what was good for the country was good for General Motors and vice versa." General Motors was so large and successful that its interests were inextricably linked with the national interest, though perhaps not quite to the degree as suggested by Wilson. But nonetheless, General Motors was the undisputed king, and it was Alfred Sloan who won them the crown.

Alfred Sloan's approach varied from his contemporary and adversary Henry Ford's, and these differences contributed significantly to the success of General Motors. Ford focused first and foremost on production efficiencies and building economies of scale. Sloan took a marketing-centric approach focused on delivering against the needs and wants of a diverse group of consumers.

Henry Ford famously proclaimed in his autobiography, "a customer can have a car painted any colour that he wants so long as it is black." Sloan believed in developing, "A car for every purse and purpose."

These philosophical differences led to vastly different go-to-market strategies for their two companies. Ford resisted the notion of planned obsolesces. Sloan embraced it and pioneered the annual styling change strategy to keep models fresh from year to year.

More importantly, Sloan developed what he called the "Ladder of Success." Under this model, General Motor's product lines had a clearly established pricing structure. From lowest to highest priced, the ladder of success included: Chevrolet, Pontiac, Oldsmobile, Buick and Cadillac.

Each division's vehicles served a different consumer – a different car for every purse. GM divisions didn't compete with each other. They built upon each other. As consumers aged and disposable income grew, they migrated upwards through the General Motors line, steadily climbing the ladder of success.

Sloan believed strongly in decentralized management with centralized control. Each division operated separately and independently, but within clearly defined and centrally planned parameters. Chevrolet would always serve the bottom end of the market and Cadillac the top, but individual division managers had autonomy to innovate and grow within those segments. They just had to abide by their centrally defined roles.

Behind Sloan's leadership GM grew fantastically for decades. At its zenith in the late-1950s, General Motors was arguably the largest and most important company in the entire world.

The Dénouement

A confluence of factors ultimately led to the demise of General Motors in 2009. The strength of foreign competition, poor labor relations, diminished product quality, economic downturns, and managerial missteps all contributed to GM's decades-long fall from grace. But the beginning of the decline started when the once independent and carefully coordinated operating divisions started to act like a selfish herd, grouping progressively tighter together when under attack.

Beginning in the late 1950s, GM started to act less like a leader and more like a reactionary follower. As competitors launched new car models, GM reacted, often poorly.

When Volkswagen launched the Beetle, GM countered with the Chevy Corvair which gained a reputation for being incredibly unsafe. To compete with new subcompact imports, GM launched a series of new models including the Chevy Vega whose production problems and labor disputes led to increased costs.

These poorly executed reactions were indicative of a deeper problem – the decline of thoughtful and coordinated decision making and the beginning of reactionary independent actions by the individual operating divisions. As the individual operating units reacted to competitive threats without centralized coordination, the cars they made started to look and perform the same. These reactionary decisions resembled the behavior of a selfish herd, and they inflicted lasting and devastating damage by undermining the ladder of success that Sloan had carefully cultivated for decades.

When the Ford Mustang grew in popularity, GM offered competing high performance vehicles in both the Chevy Camaro and the Pontiac Firebird. Both Chevy and Pontiac now offered similar higher performance engines that previously would have only been found in offerings from the higher priced divisions.

In addition to offering higher performing engines, both operating units launched new higher trim models including the Chevrolet Impala and the Pontiac Bonneville.

Chevrolets and Pontiacs were starting to look, perform, and be priced like Oldsmobiles, Buicks and Cadillacs.

Furthermore, throughout the 1960s, in response to the growing demand and foreign competition in the new compact and intermediate car markets, Pontiac, Oldsmobile and Buick each introduced similar looking and comparably priced compact cars of their own. The lines continued to blur.

At one point in 1977, due to exceptionally strong demand for its Oldsmobile product line and the resulting shortage of Oldsmobile engines, GM secretly substituted Chevrolet engines in its Oldsmobile line. Customers were shocked to find a Chevy, not an Oldsmobile engine, under the hood. It was a public relations nightmare for GM, but instead of using this as a warning signal to stop muddying up the distinctions between their product lines, the shoal of GM divisions herded ever closer together.

Instead of going back to the successful model that included division specific engines, GM started adding disclaimers to its vehicles stating that the car could include an engine produced at another GM division. Soon all GM cars would have engines that were "GM corporate engines" and "Produced by GM Power Train."

Affluent customers who wanted to buy the higher trim, higher quality, higher priced Cadillac, now had to a settle for a vehicle with the same engine as a Chevy, the car that was driven by less affluent people. Why pay more for a Cadillac or a Buick when it had the same engine as a Chevy?

The migration to the middle by the selfish herd of GM divisions didn't stop with just the engine. GM divisions started to share the same body platforms, such as the X-Body platform and J-Body platform.

By the late 1970s and prior to the recession of the early 1980s, the GM ladder of success had been all but completely destroyed. Chevrolet, Pontiac, Oldsmobile, Buick and Cadillac shared both engines and body-types. They performed the same, they looked the same, and they cost the same. There was no longer a car for every purse and every purpose. The once clear lines between the cars produced by the various GM divisions weren't just muddied, they were obliterated.

Once under attack from competition and on the defensive from self-inflicted wounds, each GM division reacted like a herding animal trying desperately to save itself. In an effort to protect their own market share, the divisions ended up trampling over each other and failing miserably.

After peaking in 1960, GM's market share fell consistently each of the next three decades. By the 1990s, GM's share had eroded to levels GM hadn't experienced since the 1920s.

Through the business cycles of the 1990s and 2000s, GM rode the peaks and valleys. But the peaks grew smaller and the valleys got deeper as the once venerable company continued to hemorrhage market share.

GM never took charge of its destiny. It never pulled apart its operating divisions and defined distinct markets or created unique roles for its brands. The selfish herd couldn't or wouldn't be torn asunder. The operating units continued to stomp all over each other.

After the retirement of Alfred Sloan and under competitive threat, the individual operating divisions of GM began to act like a selfish herd. They all started to act the same. They started to offer similar vehicles at similar prices. Sloan's carefully constructed market segmentation model and approach collapsed, crushed by the selfish herd.

On June 1, 2009, at approximately 9:00AM, General Motors, once the largest company in the world, as part of a bailout plan orchestrated by the US Treasury Department, filed for Chapter 11 Bankruptcy. Absent Sloan's leadership, GM's divisions all acted the same, they all zigged, and collectively, they failed.

CHAPTER 39

THREE MEN MAKE A TIGER

"More doctors smoke Camels than any other cigarette."

– R. J. Reynolds slogan for Camel Brand Cigarettes used in the late 1940s and 1950s

The ancient Chinese proverb known as "Three Men Make a Tiger" dates back to the Warring States period of Chinese history (475BC – 221BC). During this time, regional warlords controlled various portions of modern day China and they constantly jockeyed for territory and control.

One day, Pang Cong, a trusted advisor of the King of Wei, needed to embark on a long journey. Pang Cong feared that his adversaries would spread ugly rumors about him while he was gone and that those lies would sway the King's opinion of him. He feared that he would lose the King's trust before his return to Wei.

To convince the King to dismiss the falsehoods, Pang Cong told the King a parable called "Three Men Make a Tiger." Pang Cong asked the King, "If someone told you that a single man reported that he saw a tiger roaming freely about the marketplace, would you believe him?" The King quickly replied that he wouldn't believe the fantastical report. Pang Cong continued, "What if two people reported seeing the tiger?" Again, the King declared that he wouldn't believe such an unlikely story. Pang Cong persisted, "What if three men reported that they saw a tiger roaming freely about the marketplace?" To this final question, the King replied that he would believe the reports. If three people said they saw the tiger, then he would believe it. For the King, three men made a tiger.

Pang Cong tried desperately to convince the King that just because many people say or believe something that it doesn't make it true. He knew that people tend to believe even absurd information if enough people mention and repeat it. Pang Cong knew that if people, including the King, would believe something as ridiculous as a tiger wandering freely about the marketplace, that they would easily believe lies about him.

Pang Cong made great points to the King, but in the end, his efforts failed. While Pang Cong traveled, his adversaries spread untruths about him and the King eventually believed them. When Pang Cong finally returned home from his journey, the King refused to see him. Despite the colorful parable and the soundness of the lesson, the King still fell directly into the trap.

Pang Cong knew that people tend to change their beliefs to conform to the crowd. The more who believe, the more it must be true. Logical arguments that exploit this tendency are known as "Argumentum ad populum" or "appeal to the people." While logically flawed, they prove incredibly powerful in persuading people to change their thinking.

An argumentum ad populum might go something like "Brand A is the most popular brand, therefore it is the best" or "Most people support the proposed legislation; therefore it is a good idea and should be supported." These types of arguments abound in our daily rhetoric, marketing, and politics.

Because of its power, savvy advertising executives and politicians employ the logic of argumentum ad populum to influence their targets. These cunning manipulators leverage people's proclivity to conform to their advantage. They zag by influencing the masses to zig and do their bidding.

3 Men (Doctors) Make a Tiger (Safe Cigarette)

In 1913, R.J. Reynolds launched the Camel Brand in the United States as the first pre-packaged cigarette. Before Camel, smokers rolled their own cigarettes. This tremendous innovation greatly increased the product's convenience. R.J. Reynolds used a unique Turkish paper that inspired the Camel brand name, and, perhaps more importantly, they blended the tobacco to create a smoother, less harsh smoking experience than other offerings on the market.

Reynolds launched this innovative and differentiated new product with clever advertising. They had a live Camel wander through towns and distribute free samples. They created the iconic "I'd Walk a Mile for Camel" slogan that endured for decades. To top it off, Reynolds undercut their competitor's prices. Not surprisingly, the brand was an outstanding success. Within the first year, Reynolds sold 425 million packs.

In the late 1940s and early 50s, Camel employed a marketing campaign that capitalized on the social phenomenon described in the "Three Men Make a Tiger" parable. At the time, nascent public concern about the health risks posed by cigarettes was starting to grow. Camel sought to inoculate against this growing sales headwind, and they put their legendary marketing team to work.

The advertising team developed the insightfully devious "More Doctors Smoke Camels" campaign. And, as they usually did, the brand launched the campaign with vigor through heavy and persistent television and print advertising. The campaign's explicit claim – Camel was the brand of cigarettes preferred by doctors. The implicit claim – cigarettes must be healthy, or so many doctors wouldn't smoke them.

The campaign bears a striking similarity to the Chinese Parable – of course there is a tiger in the market, or so many people wouldn't report seeing one. Pang Cong would have been proud.

Camel used the credibility of the trusted doctor to dupe the masses into purchasing more of their cigarettes, successfully leveraging a fundamental human tendency to its advantage. They knew that people tend to conform, even to absurd beliefs, if a group shares the same idea.

I Like Ike

Dwight D. Eisenhower already completed a distinguished career before being elected the 34th President of the Unites States. After graduating from West Point, he served as Army Chief of Staff under President Harry S. Truman. During World War II, he served as a 5-star General in the US Army and Supreme Commander of all Allied forces in Europe. He led invasions in Northern Europe, France (D-Day), and Germany successfully leading the Allies to victory. After WWII, he became the first supreme commander of NATO.

Following his distinguished military career, Eisenhower decided to run for President in 1952. His campaign's research showed that people trusted and admired Eisenhower, but didn't like to discuss his views on the issues.

On the issues, many people didn't really know Eisenhower's position on them and others weren't sure they agreed wholeheartedly with them. So, instead of focusing on issues, the campaign took a classic argumentum ad populum approach – the "I Like Ike" campaign. I like Ike, everyone likes Ike, and therefore, you should too.*

The campaign plastered the now-famous slogan on all Eisenhower campaign paraphernalia, and they created six campaign busses to tour about the country to spread the message. In large bold letters, the busses read "Eisenhower Bandwagon." As the campaign toured about the country,

---

* "Ike" was Eisenhower's childhood nickname. It was originally intended as an abbreviation for his last name.

they implored people to join the crowd and support Ike. Get on the bandwagon, support Ike, everyone else likes Ike.

On November 4, 1952, Ike won a decisive victory over Democrat Adlai Stevenson to become the 34th President of The United States. He carried 39 states and won the electoral vote by a commanding 442 to 89 margin.

Indeed, the country liked Ike.

Since the approach worked so well in 1952, the 1956 Eisenhower Reelection Campaign followed a similar strategy: "I Still Like Ike."

It worked equally well. Eisenhower defeated Adlai Stevenson again, this time by a slightly larger margin in the Electoral College, 457-73.

Like Camel's advertising team, the Eisenhower campaign leveraged humanity's drive to conform to their advantage. People often conform and think and act just like everyone else because they want to be just like everyone else. They do certain things and believe certain things because that is what everyone else does and everyone else believes. They just want to get on the bandwagon. And they will believe almost anything – provided that enough other people do too.

Camel duped the masses into purchasing more of their cigarettes. Eisenhower gained election to the Presidency. Both zagged by acting like the dolphins that cut the great shoal into bait balls by cleverly utilizing people's tendencies to their advantage.

CHAPTER 40

CONSENSUS AT ANY COST

> *"A 'collective' mind does not exist. It is merely the sum of endless numbers of individual minds. If we have an endless number of individual minds who are weak, meek, submissive and impotent – who renounce their creative supremacy for the sake of the 'whole' and accept humbly that the 'whole's' verdict – we don't get a collective super-brain. We get only the weak, meek, submissive and impotent collective mind."*
>
> – Ayn Rand

Research psychologist Irving Janus coined the term "Groupthink" to describe the phenomenon when a group's desire for conformity results in dysfunctional decision making. In an effort to minimize conflict and reach consensus, group members fail to evaluate alternative choices and discount contrarian perspectives. Conformity supersedes individual and divergent thinking, and as a result, groups reach faulty decisions.

To understand groupthink, consider the failed attempt to overthrow Cuban Prime Minister Fidel Castro known as the Bay of Pigs fiasco. During the Eisenhower administration, the CIA developed plans for the invasion. After Kennedy's election, his new administration quickly and without critical evaluation accepted the established plan and began to move headlong toward executing the attack.

Before the invasion, the Administration received evidence that someone leaked details of the plan. Despite this revelation, the tight-knit group proceeded, downplaying the implications of a security breach.

They also minimized concerns about the soundness of the plan. Two members of Kennedy's planning team Arthur Schlesinger Jr. and Senator J. William Fulbright each voiced uncertainty about pressing forward, but their attempts fell on deaf ears. Other members staunchly defended and rationalized the plan. Eventually, the dissenting voices grew softer as they discounted their individual concerns and acquiesced to the group's perspective. To avoid conflict, the group drove to consensus.

The planning committee made several critical errors including underestimating the strength of Castro's forces. And they could have and should have critically questioned several other aspects of the plan. But when some dissented, the group continued to drive toward consensus, quickly and summarily dismissing any objections.

They ignored the possibility of a leak. They downplayed concerns about the plan. They silenced dissenting voices. And acting on a perceived moral obligation, they launched the compromised and poorly planned invasion.

On April 17, 1961, a CIA-trained group of Cuban exiles funded and supported by the United States government invaded Southern Cuba. It took Castro's forces just three days to thwart the invasion and thoroughly embarrass the United States and President Kennedy.

The Bay of Pigs fiasco shares several similarities to the United States' failure to anticipate and prepare for the Japanese attack on Pearl Harbor nearly two decades earlier. In the months leading up to the attack, the officers in command of the US base held a strong and prevailing belief that the Japanese would not dare launch an attack at Pearl Harbor. But just prior to the attack, United States intelligence intercepted secret messages that indicated that Japan intended to attack Pearl Harbor.

Commanders in Washington sent warning to the remote base, but the officers in charge dismissed the communication. The group already reached a strong consensus. They were certain that Japan would never attack.

When confronted with the news from Washington, the officers developed rationalizations to preserve the already established consensus. Japan will never attack. An attack would lead to an all-out war that they would certainly lose. Even if they attack, we would easily thwart it.

The officers who believed the warning from Washington didn't speak up. They feared rocking the boat and harsh scrutiny from challenging the consensus. The officers' drive to maintain a group consensus proved extremely costly. On December 7, 1941, the Imperial Japanese Navy attacked Pearl Harbor and destroyed 188 US aircraft and killed 2,402 Americans.

In Janus' seminal work, he identified three antecedent conditions that foster groupthink. The first condition is "high group cohesiveness." The more cohesive the group, the more likely that group will succumb to groupthink.

Consider the Kennedy administration prior to Bay of Pigs invasion. Powerful social forces including common political affiliations bound that group tightly together. Similarly, the officers at Pearl Harbor formed a highly cohesive group unified by military conditioning and a common purpose. Both highly cohesive groups stifled dissenting views promoting groupthink.

Janus believed "situational context" the next most important condition. Situations involving highly stressful external threats and situations posing moral dilemmas tend to exacerbate groupthink. In the Bay of Pigs example, the Kennedy administration believed overthrowing Castro was a moral obligation. In the Pearl Harbor example, the external threat posed by the Japanese made the US officers entrench more deeply into their previously held consensus.

Janus identified "structural faults" with team construction as the third antecedent condition. Highly isolated groups lacking impartial leadership and consisting of members with homogeneous social backgrounds dramatically increases the likelihood of problems. The Kennedy Administration had an agenda. The Naval officers shared highly similar backgrounds.

These two examples highlight the risks associated with group formation. Group work isn't necessarily a bad thing. Pooling people with diverse ideas and experiences can ultimately lead to better decisions. But under certain circumstances, poorly formed and ineffectively led groups create a crucible for groupthink.

Highly cohesive groups with structural flaws operating under pressure frequently creates groupthink. In these situations, the group member's desire for harmony prevails, resulting in an unfortunate choice of conformity over conflict. With groupthink, the primary motivation is conflict avoidance, not reaching the best decision. Regrettably, the drive to conform overpowers the individual and they acquiesce to the group position to avoid arguments and disagreements with their group members.*

---

* Fortunately, leaders can employ several methods for avoiding groupthink. They can build diverse teams with impartial leaders who don't express their opinion too soon or forcefully guide the group to consensus. Leaders should encourage critical thinking, objections, and the evaluation of all alternatives. And they should assign at least one member of the group the role of Devil's Advocate. Leaders should also ensure groups remain connected to people outside the team by encouraging members to speak with trusted outsiders or by bringing external experts into the group.

CHAPTER 41

THE DEVIL'S ADVOCATE

"Saints should always be judged guilty until they are proved innocent."

– George Orwell

The Roman Catholic Church follows an extensive process known as canonization to officially declare a deceased person a saint. By designating someone a saint, the Church officially pronounces that it believes the person lived and died in an exemplary and holy way and the person now rests in heaven.

Once canonized, the person gains inclusion in the official liturgy or worship of the church and can be included in prayers including a sacred prayer known as the Litany of the Saints. The church also grants the newly minted saint a feast day in their honor. The Church can name individual churches after the saint. And church members can publicly venerate their likeness or their relics via bowing or making the sign of the cross.* Becoming a saint is a tremendous and extremely rare honor, and accordingly, the Catholic Church takes the process very seriously.

Over the millennia, the canonization process has changed significantly, but the final decision making body has remained constant. The final decision rests with the Holy See, the diocese or district of the Catholic Church in Rome. Most know the leader of this diocese by his more common name – The Pope. And he is the unquestioned leader of the worldwide Roman Catholic Church.

While the ultimate canonization decision rests with the Holy See, a lengthy process precedes the final determination. To be considered for sainthood, a person must have lived an incredibly virtuous and faithful life, and church members must actively champion his or her candidacy throughout the process. The Church must believe and formally recognize that person has entered into heaven and either died as a martyr or performed a miracle. The Catholic Church calls this step beatification, a very rare and incredibly blessed honor.

After beatification, and before one can gain recognition as a saint, it must be proven that the person performed another miracle. Once the Church recognizes a second miracle, the Pope may declare the person a saint, and the entire church must accept the declaration as infallible. †

---

* In Roman Catholic teaching, veneration is a distinct honor that falls just short of adoration which is the act of worship reserved for God alone.

† In Roman Catholic teaching, the doctrine of papal infallibility states that the Pope cannot make an error when speaking ex cathedra (literally "from the Chair" referring to the chair of the first Pope, Saint

Proving that a person lived a virtuous life and their soul now rests in heaven requires great effort. Proving that same person performed not one, but rather two miracles is exceedingly difficult. These are incredibly difficult decisions fraught with uncertainty. Yet, this is the task the Roman Catholic Church faces when deciding to canonize a prospective saint.

The decision faced by the Church is challenging and important, and the dynamics of the situation create a crucible for groupthink. Examining the group dynamics and decision at hand using Janus' antecedent condition as a framework illuminates the high potential for groupthink:

> Highly Cohesive Group: Yes. The Holy See is an incredibly cohesive group bound tightly together by a strongly held faith and common purpose. Additionally, the group places an incredibly high value on hierarchy and includes rigid and clearly defined roles amongst the clergy.

> Situational Context: Yes. The situation is charged with moral implications including determination of another person's virtue, their place in heaven or hell, and their ability to perform miracles.

Peter) when he solemnly declares a dogmatic teaching on matters of faith. It doesn't mean, as many assume, that the Pope is always correct, even when speaking on matters of official church business, or that he cannot sin or err in his personal life.

<u>Structural Faults</u>: Yes. An incredibly homogeneous group consisting of similarly aged men sharing the same exact occupation, lifestyle, and faith. Additionally, the group is often extremely isolated, especially when engaging in important decisions, and lacks impartial leadership. In fact, the Pope, who functions as the leader, often has a vested interest in the outcome having nominated or supported the candidate for sainthood himself. Moreover, an actual doctrine of the group holds that in certain situations the leader, the Pope, speaks as a direct mouthpiece of God and is completely infallible. Group members believe that to question the Pope on certain matters of faith is equivalent to questioning the God they worship.

Centuries before Janus coined the term groupthink, Pope Sixtus V understood the difficulty of the situation facing the Church. In 1587, to inoculate against biased decision making, Pope Sixtus V created a new position called the "Promoter of the Faith." Later, the Church would call this person the "Devil's Advocate."

During the canonization process, the Devil's Advocate's job was to argue against the canonization of the prospective saint. They took a skeptical view of the way the person lived their life and critically investigated the evidence that supported the miracles they were said to have performed.

Long before Janus, the Catholic Church took tangible and successful steps to guard against groupthink. Because of Pope Sixtus V's creation, the Roman Catholic Church successfully managed the canonization process without errantly driving to consensus in favor of sainthood.

That all changed in 1983 when Pope John Paul II reformed the canonization process and made the role of the Promoter of the Faith less adversarial. This allowed groupthink to proliferate and thrive in the canonization process.

Even after accounting for his long tenure, Pope John Paul II's canonization and beatification totals were remarkable.* During his reign, the Church canonized 482 as saints and beatified 1,338 more – both far and away the most in Church history. For perspective, the seven other Popes who served during the 20th century only accounted for 98 canonizations combined. And the 1,338 beatifications exceed the combined total of the 37 Popes in the nearly 400 years since Pope Sixtus V held the office.

Effectively removing the Devil's Advocate unleashed an unprecedented wave of Canonizations and Beatifications. Were more miracles worked by people who died during or just before Pope John Paul II was elected Pope? Did people live more virtuous, righteous, and holy lives? Or, did groupthink among the Holy See accelerate with the removal of the Devil's advocate leading to an unprecedented drive to consensus in line with the wishes of Pope John Paul II?

---

* At 26 years and 168 days, Pope John Paul II's tenure was the second longest in Church history.

CHAPTER 42

HOW VASILI ARKHIPOV SAVED THE WORLD

"A guy called Vasili Arkhipov saved the world."

— Thomas Blanton, Director of the National Security Archive, a non-profit organization that archives and publishes declassified United States Government information obtained through the Freedom of Information Act

In October 1962, the world stood at a standstill on the precipice of full scale nuclear war as the two great superpowers, the United States and the Soviet Union, engaged in a nerve-racking standoff known as the Cuban Missile Crisis. The tense confrontation that lasted 13 days marked a high-water mark in the Cold War. And it was the closest that the world has come to nuclear holocaust and complete annihilation of civilization.

By late 1962, and despite Kennedy's strongest efforts and desires, the United States had failed to overthrow Fidel Castro's communist regime in Cuba. The botched Bay of

Pigs invasion cost the United States and President Kennedy credibility. Other Kennedy sanctioned efforts to spark revolt and oust Castro, including Project Mongoose, had failed.

Emboldened by the US failures and believing that Kennedy lacked the experience and decisiveness necessary to successfully manage crisis, Nikita Khrushchev and the Soviets embarked on a course of action they had not considered seriously with President Eisenhower in office.

Starting in July 1962, Soviet construction teams began the installation of nuclear missiles in Cuba. With Cuban leader Fidel Castro's blessing, the Soviets secretly positioned and camouflaged enough nuclear missiles to destroy the majority of the United States of America.

Prior to the build-up in Cuba, the Soviets lacked sufficient intercontinental ballistic missile capability to act as a credible "mutual destruction" deterrent against a United States attack. They had nuclear capability to obliterate United States allies across Europe and target large sections of the continental US. But the Soviets lacked the capability to accurately target all major US cities with the complete certainty of total destruction that Khrushchev coveted.

At the time, the United States had a significant nuclear weapons capability in Europe including an arsenal of missiles in Italy and Turkey that could completely annihilate Moscow within 16 minutes of launch. By building nuclear capability in Cuba that could reliably destroy New York and Washington DC, Khrushchev believed he could create "A balance of fear." That balance would create deterrence which would create peace while simultaneously protecting the strategically important communist regime in Cuba.

Despite the Soviets best efforts to covertly install the weaponry, United States intelligence operatives learned about the build-up and informed their superiors. Intelligence officials initially dismissed the reports from the field. But eventually, on October 14th, U-2 aerial reconnaissance photographs of Cuba captured images of the Soviet missiles in Cuba. The next day, the CIA reviewed the photographs, confirmed that Soviet nukes were in Cuba, and informed President Kennedy. The Cuban Missile Crisis had begun.

To Kennedy's credit, he learned from his failures during the Bay of Pigs situation. During that debacle, Kennedy and team fell into the trap of groupthink and plunged headlong into an embarrassing and costly decision. During the Cuban Missile Crisis, Kennedy showed both wisdom and restraint in averting thermonuclear war. However, his approach would lead to a tense standoff with the Soviets.

Kennedy and his team, a group known as the Executive Committee of the National Security Council, evaluated a wide range of potential responses to the Soviet build up in Cuba. The options ranged from doing absolutely nothing to a full-scale invasion of Cuba which would have likely precipitated World War III.

Despite dissenting opinions from the Joint Chiefs of Staff who favored an all-out invasion, Kennedy opted for a naval blockade of Cuba. The blockade plan involved utilizing US military forces to effectively "quarantine"

Cuba, preventing any additional weapons from entering the island nation.

Once the US established the blockade, they would demand that the Soviets dismantle their military bases and nuclear weaponry in Cuba before lifting the "quarantine." The Kennedy team only held onto slight hope that the Soviets would acquiesce to their demands, but the blockade provided a superior option to initiating an attack that would culminate in World War.

On October 22nd, Kennedy addressed his nation informing the citizens of the United States of the presence of Soviet missiles in Cuba and the United States plan to quarantine the island. With the US blockade plan in place, the ball was in Khrushchev's court.

Publicly, Khrushchev and the Soviets proclaimed the US blockade in international waters an act of aggression, akin to the actions of "pirates." Secretly, employing back channel communications with President Kennedy, Khrushchev worked to develop an amicable solution.

Working to diffuse the situation that his actions precipitated, Khrushchev wrote to Kennedy, eloquently offering the following plea:

Mr. President, we and you ought not now to pull on the ends of the rope in which you have tied the knot of war, because the more the two of us pull, the tighter that knot will be tied. And a moment may come when that knot will be tied so tight that even he who tied it will not have the strength to untie it, and then it will be necessary to cut that knot, and what that would mean is not for me to explain to you, because you yourself understand perfectly of what terrible forces our countries dispose.

Consequently, if there is no intention to tighten that knot and thereby to doom the world to the catastrophe of thermonuclear war, then let us not only relax the forces pulling on the ends of the rope, let us take measures to untie that knot. We are ready for this.

The back-channel negotiations between Kennedy and Khrushchev continued, eventually culminating with public meetings and a compromise that would diffuse the powder keg that threatened to explode in Cuba and destroy the entire world.

Publicly, the Soviets agreed to dismantle their missiles in Cuba and the Americans vowed to never again invade the island nation. Additionally, the two countries established a nuclear hotline to directly link current and future US Presidents and Soviet leaders to help avert future crises. The United States agreed to remove nuclear missiles positioned in Turkey and Italy. And, to his credit, Khrushchev permitted the US to dismantle in secret at great expense to his political capital as the offer created the illusion that he lost the negotiations with Kennedy.

On November 20, 1962, the US lifted the quarantine of Cuba ending the Cuban Missile Crisis. The leaders of the two superpowers partnered to untie the knot of war that they helped tie in the first place. Crisis was averted and nuclear holocaust remained only a nightmare, not a reality. But, at the time, not even Kennedy or Khrushchev knew how closely their nations came to nuclear war. And to this day, most only know the lead players who helped avert catastrophe, but few know the name of Vasili Arkhipov, the man who saved the world.

Vasili Arkhipov

Vasili Arkhipov was born into a peasant family just outside of Moscow. He was given a military education that prepared him to serve his country. And he served his country, and his world, with honor.

A little over a year before the Cuban Missile Crisis, in July 1961, Arkhipov served as deputy commander on a nuclear powered and nuclear missile equipped submarine known as the K-19. While conducting exercises off the coast of Greenland, the cooling system developed a major leak. Unfortunately for the crew, the submarine lacked a back-up cooling system. Unless the crew could fix the leak, the reactor would melt down causing a terrible disaster.

Arkhipov lent his engineering expertise to the team that fought through deadly radiation to stop the leak. Several workers died within days of the incident. This nearly led to a mutiny on a nuclear powered and nuclear equipped submarine on the verge of nuclear meltdown. Arkhipov's support for the captain and calm bravery under extreme duress helped quell the mutiny. For his leadership, Arkhipov earned a medal for bravery, but more importantly, he earned the enduring respect of his fellow sailors and invaluable experience in managing through crisis.

Arkhipov served his native Soviet Union bravely and with honor earning him great respect. He would need all that respect and crisis management experience when he served all of humanity one fateful day on October 27, 1962 at the apex of the Cuban Missile Crisis.

With Kennedy and Khrushchev embroiled in crisis, publicly posturing and secretly negotiating above ground, Arkhipov was trapped in a nuclear-armed Soviet Foxtrot class B-59 submarine off the shores of Cuba. Arkhipov was second in charge.

In preparation for thermonuclear war, the Soviets equipped the submarine with nuclear tipped torpedoes, and the three officers on board were given a strict protocol on when they could deploy the devastating weapons. The officers could only launch nuclear weapons if given direct orders from Moscow or if all three officers, including Arkhipov, unanimously agreed to deploy.

On October 27th, eleven US Navy destroyers and a US aircraft carrier had located and pinned Arkhipov's submarine deep underwater. The communication link on the Soviet submarine had been damaged, preventing the trapped commanders from connecting with Moscow. They had no way to get information on the situation or receive orders on how to proceed.

With their quarry pinned deep in Caribbean waters, the US forces started to drop depth charges trying to force the Soviet sub to surface. Trapped, cut-off from Moscow, and on the brink of nuclear war, the three Soviet officers faced a decision that would define the future of humanity.

Should they surface and surrender or should they launch an attack?

And they would need to make the decision under conditions that created a crucible for groupthink:

Highly Cohesive Group: It was an incredibly cohesive group. The three officers were all members of the same country, the same military force, and on the same crew. They lived together in an airtight submarine. They trained together, they fought together, and they were prepared to die together.

Situational Context: The Cuban Missile Crisis may have been the most stressful and tense situation in human history. The crew hadn't heard from Moscow in days. They were cornered by a fleet of enemy ships who were dropping explosive devices into the water above their trapped submarine. In the middle of a nuclear standoff and under threat from a clear and present danger, the situation couldn't have been more stressful. The crew faced a terrible predicament – completely isolated, under attack, and possibly already engaged in nuclear war.

Structural Faults: The group was extremely homogeneous being comprised of entirely Soviet Naval personnel with highly similar social backgrounds and political ideologies. They shared a pervasive belief in the moral supremacy of communism over democracy. And the isolation of the group couldn't have been more extreme. They were locked in an airtight submarine under the water, completely disconnected from the outside world.

In this petri dish of conditions ideal for propagating groupthink, three officers needed to make a decision that would alter the course of history. Launch a nuclear weapon? Or surface to face the enemy?

The submarine's captain Valentin Savitsky advocated launching a nuclear-tipped torpedo. Having not heard from Moscow in days and facing fire from the Americans, he believed that nuclear war had already commenced and that his submarine should join in the fight. In his view, surfacing would lead to capture and an abdication of his duty to defend his native land in a war with the Americans. Specifically, he advocated launching a 10-kiloton nuclear torpedo at the USS Randolph, the US aircraft carrier that had the Soviet sub pinned below the surface.

The second officer in the triumvirate was the Political Officer. He was charged with ensuring loyalty to the government and guarding against political and organizational revolution of any kind. He was completely loyal to the Soviet Union, and his ideological post required him to demand similar loyalty from the others on board. He, like the Captain, advocated launching the nuclear-tipped torpedo.

If they launched the torpedo, nuclear war would have quickly spread around the globe. The United States would have countered with strikes on Moscow or Cuba. The Soviets would have responded by wiping out US allies, airbases, and troop concentrations across Europe. England, Germany, Turkey, and Italy would have been targeted and obliterated.

Unbeknownst to US military officials at the time, the United States lacked the ability to stop missiles in Cuba from destroying the United States mainland. US officials possessed deeply flawed intelligence reports on the Soviet capability in Cuba. They didn't know the location of scores of nuclear weapons and severely underestimated the Soviet troop presence. They didn't know about the tactical nuclear weapons that would have vaporized any amphibious force immediately upon landing on Cuba's sugar-white beaches. The United States would have been annihilated.

Arkhipov's captain had given the order to fire a nuclear weapon. The Political Officer concurred. Under attack, possibly already in a thermonuclear war, Vasili Arkhipov had to make the most important decision of his life.

In a similar situation, boiling in a cauldron of groupthink, most men would choose to conform. They would fall in line with their fellow officers, choosing to reach consensus. They would zig and choose to join the shoal.

But Vasili Arkhipov was not most men. He opposed his fellow officers. He pleaded with them to surface and contact Moscow before launching a nuclear attack. Eventually, Savitsky relented. He agreed to surface the submarine and contact Moscow.

The world came closer to thermonuclear annihilation than most realize. One man refused to conform and singlehandedly prevented World War III.

Vasili Arkhipov bravely chose to zag, and in so doing, Vasili Arkhipov saved the world.

Post Script

People conform for a variety of reasons. Sometimes people conform to avoid conflict or embarrassment. Other times, people conform by acting on instinct like a herd of animals. Occasionally, people will conform because they want to be like everyone else.

To conquer the enemy of conformity that sucks people into the shoal, one must rebel against the conventional. One must derive their own wisdom and act on their own volition. Only then, can one zag.

PART SEVEN

PARTING SHOTS

CHAPTER 43

GOOD ISN'T BAD

"Don't reinvent the wheel."

– Some Caveman

For the individual sardine, the instinct to join a shoal and follow every other sardine serves it well for most of its life. The shoal brings it food and safety. It provides access to mates and makes swimming easier. For its entire life with the exception of one fateful day, the sardine benefitted from membership in the collective.

In the simple sardine shoal metaphor, zigging refers to mindlessly following the shoal and behaving exactly the same way as every member of the group. Translating to human behavior, the concept of zigging applies more broadly, and with more complexity, but the core idea remains the same.

Human "zigging" includes all conventional thinking and behavior. It means thinking the way others think and doing things the "normal" way in a manner that most wouldn't think to question. These conventional approaches are deeply ingrained, and in some cases, they are hardwired into our brains before we are born. Since people share similar tendencies, people tend to think and act in the same way. And most of the time, as with the sardines, this works out for the best.

Zigging offers many benefits. For a society to function properly and its members to thrive, individuals must zig and conform consistently and along numerous dimensions. For example, agreeing to drive on the same side of the road keeps people safe and obeying the rule of law enables a civilization, and its citizens, to prosper.

In addition to keeping people safe and serving as the backbone of civilization, zigging offers an efficient and effective approach for most people. Oftentimes making thoughtless decisions makes perfectly good sense. The economic concept known as rational ignorance holds that in some situations, the cost of educating oneself on an issue exceeds the potential benefit that improved information and the optimal decision would yield.

Consider the decision of which brand of toothpaste to purchase. The choice comes down to two well-known and respected brands that offer a similar list of benefits and credentials. While one brand is probably slightly better for your specific situation, and there is probably a marginally better choice to make, the cost to make the perfect decision outweighs the potential benefit of making the perfect choice.

You could read the entire label on each product, call your dentist, call another dentist or two for a second and third opinion, research the two products online, and call each company and request information and a sample. You could call the local university and speak to the professor who heads the dental department. You could invest heavily and make the perfect decision for you.

Or, you could just pick one of the two incredibly similar brands and move on to the next item on your shopping list. Most choose the latter option, and according to the concept of rational ignorance, they are making a wise choice.

Conventional wisdom usually becomes collectively accepted because it works reasonably well most of the time. With limited time and resources, people need to follow the crowd from time to time. If they don't, they'll be stuck in a quagmire of never ending analysis, paralyzed, and unable to make it past even the simplest of tasks such as choosing a brand of toothpaste.

Conventional approaches capitalize on the cumulative knowledge of society, and more often than not, generate correct decisions and acceptable results. There is often no need to reinvent the wheel when the wheel you have works just fine.

Benefitting from the collective wisdom of others isn't just something relegated to selecting a brand of toothpaste. People follow the crowd and watch the most popular TV shows, frequent the same popular restaurants, and drive the same popular car brands. Most of the time, this works out just fine for the imitator as the most popular TV shows, restaurants, and cars are often very good, or at least the ones that meet the average person's tastes and preferences the best.

Moreover, people continually share advice and learn from each other. Family recipes are passed down from grandmother to mother to grandchild. The notion of each successive generation creating their own recipe sounds foolish – and it is. Continually reinventing the wheel or Grandma Opel's Apple Pie over and over again is a waste of time.

Mental shortcuts or heuristics prove the economical choice in a wide variety of situations. From deciding what to buy, whom to vote for, and whom to befriend, simple heuristics enable efficient decision making.

When parents implore their children to "not judge a book by its cover" when choosing friends or making other decisions, they may be teaching a good moral lesson, but not a practical one. In a complex world with limited time and capacity available to evaluate every alternative for every choice, people must judge the proverbial book by its cover – there just isn't enough time to read every book in its entirety.

When everyone else is doing something, and achieving good results, joining the shoal is often just good common sense. In these situations, zigging is both efficient and effective. People need to zig to survive and thrive – just like the sardines.

Even the greatest zaggers of all time, zig the majority of the time. Einstein stopped at red lights and probably purchased the leading brand of toothpaste and frequented popular restaurants. Newton and Galileo followed the majority of their society's laws.

But the greatest zaggers didn't follow the crowd or the conventional wisdom all of the time. Unlike the sardine that stuck with the shoal all the way until the bitter end, the great zaggers make a thoughtful choice to break free from the collective and go their own way with the expectation of success.

On balance, like with the sardines, thinking conventionally and zigging often benefits the members of the group, and it can deliver good results. Good results aren't bad. They are completely acceptable most of the time. But good isn't great. And if one ever aspires to achieve individual success or contribute to the progress of society, he or she must be willing to break from the shoal and zag.

CHAPTER 44

THE PATH TO GREATNESS

"Do not go where the path may lead, go instead where there is no path and leave a trail."

– Ralph Waldo Emerson

Zagging is the path one must pave if one aspires to achieve greatness. But it is a tough and difficult path to choose. As Einstein noted, "It takes a touch of genius – and a lot of courage to move in the opposite direction."

To zag one must make a difficult choice – a choice to break from the shoal and away from the comfortable, predictable, and often acceptable pattern of thinking and behaving conventionally. And this must be done with the expectation of success, not just the intent to be different.

Zaggers aren't simple contrarians. Thinking back to the sardine metaphor, a contrarian sardine never joins the shoal and fails to reap the benefits that group membership confers. The sardine that zags joins the shoal, reaps the benefits of membership, but then thoughtfully and boldly chooses to break from the shoal prior to embarking on the great run.

Zaggers think and act differently at the precise time and manner they think deviating from the masses will generate success. Einstein stopped at red lights, but challenged long held conventional beliefs in theoretical physics because he knew he was right. In Super Bowl XLIV, Sean Payton acted conventionally by kicking deep 6 times that day, but when he believed the moment was right and he expected success, he bravely chose to zag and execute the surprise onside kick. Vasili Arkhipov followed the conventional rules and procedures of the Soviet military most days, but he didn't succumb to groupthink and saved the world.

Great zaggers don't think and act differently all the time. They think and act differently when they expect taking a new path will yield the best results.

Zagging is hard. It requires one to overcome powerful, often instinctual or deeply ingrained forces that drive people to think and act similarly.

Mental inertia paralyzes thinking requiring a paradigm shift to achieve progress. Risk avoidance and aversion binds us to the shoal with fear necessitating bravery to "go for it" and take a calculated risk. Culture blinds individuals and skews their perceptions about the world. One must gain awareness of these second nature influences before taking action.

People have evolved to function effectively with incomplete information, but mental shortcuts and rapid cognition often result in common mistakes. Leveraging information asymmetries to one's advantage and acquiring more data to inform decisions offers great benefit. But people need to be careful not to drown in the data they covet or become paralyzed like Aesop's cunning fox.

Herding instincts, crowd psychology and groupthink can lead to conformity. The successful zagger critically questions conventional thinking, especially when he or she sees everyone else swimming along mindlessly in the same direction.

To overcome one's limitations, one must first know them. Understanding the powerful forces that bind people to the metaphorical shoal is critical to realizing one's fullest potential. To zag, one must overcome those drives and act differently than our inner wiring and external conditioning compels.

The challenge is hard, but the rewards are great. And they can be achieved.

Sardines must spend their entire life in the shoal. Instinct, not thought, governs their every action. Fortunately, people do not have to spend their entire life in the shoal. We have the ability to break free and choose to zag.

People have the power to make choices and decide what to think and how to act. People do not have to be slaves to nature or nurture. People do not have to be mindless drones destined to follow the collective. People can choose to go where there is no path and leave a trail.

People can zag. You can zag.

But to leave a trail, one must go first – don't wait.

And to leave a trail, one must find a new direction to travel – think differently.

The old adage is wrong. Great minds don't think alike. Great minds think differently. And when they recognize an opportunity to break free from the shoal and achieve success, great minds zag.

ACKNOWLEDGEMENTS

I would like to extend a special note of gratitude to all that created and provided the images used in this book.

- Chapter 4
    - Adelson Checkershadow: ©1995, Edward H. Adelson.
    - Adelson Checkershadow (Modified): ©1995, Edward H. Adelson.
- Chapter 9
    - Duck-Rabbit: Jastrow, J. (1899). The mind's eye. Popular Science Monthly, 54, 299-312.
- Chapter 21
    - Tree/Family Illusion: Unknown, possibly Robert Laws
    - Michigan Fish Test: The University of Michigan Institute for Social Research
- Chapter 27
    - Milgram Diagram: Stanley Milgram, modified by Fred the Oyster [CC BY-SA 4.0 (http://creativecommons.org/licenses/by-sa/4.0)], via Wikimedia Commons.
- Chapter 29
    - Lincoln and Mona Lisa Portraits: Original are in public domain, modified images are author's own work.
    - Dalmatian Gestalt: Unknown
    - Kanizsa Triangle: By Fibonacci (Own work) [GFDL (http://www.gnu.org/copyleft/fdl.html) or CC-BY-SA-3.0 (http://creativecommons.org/licenses/by-sa/3.0/)], via Wikimedia Commons
    - Three Dimensional Sphere: By The original uploader was Slehar at English Wikipedia (Transferred

ACKNOWLEDGEMENTS

from en.wikipedia to Commons.) [Public domain or Public domain], via Wikimedia Commons
- Ehrenstein Illusion (Left): By Nevit Dilmen (Own Drawing) [GFDL http://www.gnu.org/copyleft/fdl.html) , CC-BY-SA-3.0 (http://creativecommons.org/licenses/by-sa/3.0/) or GFDL (http://www.gnu.org/copyleft/fdl.html)], via Wikimedia Commons
- Ehrenstein Illusion (Right): By Original author is w:en:User:Tavilis (Transferred from w:en:Image:Ehrenstein2.gif) [GFDL (http://www.gnu.org/copyleft/fdl.html), CC-BY-SA-3.0 (http://creativecommons.org/licenses/by-sa/3.0/), GFDL (http://www.gnu.org/copyleft/fdl.html) or CC-BY-SA-3.0 (http://creativecommons.org/licenses/by-sa/3.0/)], via Wikimedia Commons
- Native American with an iPod: Google Maps 50°0'38.20"N 110°6'48.32"W
- Man on Mars: By Viking 1, NASA [Public domain], via Wikimedia Commons
- Dinosaur Lake in Zagreb, Croatia: Google Maps: 45.78231 N, 16.024332 E

- Chapter 33
  - Page Rank: By en:User:345Kai, User:Stannered [Public domain], via Wikimedia Commons
- Chapter 36
  - Asch Conformity Lines: By Fred the Oyster [GFDL (http://www.gnu.org/copyleft/fdl.html) or CC BY-SA 4.0-3.0-2.5-2.0-1.0 (http://creativecommons.org/licenses/by-sa/4.0-3.0-2.5-2.0-1.0)], via Wikimedia Commons

Thank You

Thank you for reading. I really hope you enjoyed it.

If you did, I would greatly appreciate it if you submitted a review on Amazon or Goodreads.

On the other hand, if you hated the book, no need to submit a review!

Contact Me

If you want to connect and talk about the book, please email me at MichaelClawsonZag@gmail.com. I'd love to hear from you.

www.ingramcontent.com/pod-product-compliance
Lightning Source LLC
Chambersburg PA
CBHW020727180526
45163CB00001B/145